Measurement and Internal Audit

Andrew Fight

■ Fast track route to mastering the principles of audit and measurement

■ Covers the key areas of internal audit from ISO 9000 certification and organisation and organising internal controls to objective setting and performance measurement systems and the impact of the Internet as a communications tool

■ Examples and lessons from some of the world's most successful public administrations and businesses, including ISO (International Organization for Standardisation), the EU Audit Control and Monitoring Directorates, OCC (Office of the Comptroller of the Currency), and ideas and case studies from auditing firms including key auditing checklists

■ Includes a glossary of key concepts and a comprehensive resources guide

OPERATIONS

06.09

>>EXPRESS EXEC.COM<<
essential management thinking at your fingertips

Copyright © Capstone Publishing 2002

The right of Andrew Fight to be identified as the author of this work has been asserted in accordance with the Copyright, Designs and Patents Act 1988

First published 2002 by
Capstone Publishing (a Wiley company)
8 Newtec Place
Magdalen Road
Oxford OX4 1RE
United Kingdom
http://www.capstoneideas.com

All rights reserved. Except for the quotation of short passages for the purposes of criticism and review, no part of this publication may be reproduced, stored in a retrieval system, or transmitted, in any form or by any means, electronic, mechanical, photocopying, recording or otherwise, without the prior permission of the publisher.

CIP catalogue records for this book are available from the British Library and the US Library of Congress

ISBN 1-84112-401-X

FSC
Mixed Sources
Product group from well-managed
forests and other controlled sources
Cert no. SGS-COC-2953
www.fsc.org
© 1996 Forest Stewardship Council

Substantial discounts on bulk quantities of Capstone books are available to corporations, professional associations and other organizations. Please contact Capstone for more details on +44 (0)1865 798 623 or (fax) +44 (0)1865 240 941 or (e-mail) info@wiley-capstone.co.uk

Contents

Introduction to ExpressExec   v

06.09.01 Introduction to Internal Audit and Measurement   1
06.09.02 What is Internal Audit, Measurement, and
          Control?   7
06.09.03 Evolution of Internal Audit and Measurement   11
06.09.04 The E-Dimension   15
06.09.05 The Global Dimension   25
06.09.06 The State of the Art – Internal Control and
          Derivatives   29
06.09.07 Internal Audit and Measurement Success Stories   39
06.09.08 Key Concepts and Thinkers   53
06.09.09 Resources   83
06.09.10 Ten Steps to Making Internal Audit and
          Measurement Work   89

Frequently Asked Questions (FAQs)   95
Index   97

Introduction to ExpressExec

ExpressExec is 3 million words of the latest management thinking compiled into 10 modules. Each module contains 10 individual titles forming a comprehensive resource of current business practice written by leading practitioners in their field. From brand management to balanced scorecard, ExpressExec enables you to grasp the key concepts behind each subject and implement the theory immediately. Each of the 100 titles is available in print and electronic formats.

Through the ExpressExec.com Website you will discover that you can access the complete resource in a number of ways:

» printed books or e-books;
» e-content – PDF or XML (for licensed syndication) adding value to an intranet or Internet site;
» a corporate e-learning/knowledge management solution providing a cost-effective platform for developing skills and sharing knowledge within an organization;
» bespoke delivery – tailored solutions to solve your need.

Why not visit www.expressexec.com and register for free key management briefings, a monthly newsletter and interactive skills checklists. Share your ideas about ExpressExec and your thoughts about business today.

Please contact elound@wiley-capstone.co.uk for more information.

Introduction to Internal Audit and Measurement

» What is audit and internal control?
» New concepts.
» Summary.

"Alice: Would you tell me, please, which way I ought to go from here?
Cat: That depends a great deal on where you want to get to."

Lewis Carroll

WHAT IS AUDIT AND INTERNAL CONTROL?

Audit and internal control basically relates to the management and control of contemporary businesses. A definition of internal auditing is provided as follows:

"Internal auditing is an independent, objective assurance and consulting activity designed to add value and improve an organization's operations. It helps an organization accomplish its objectives by bringing a systematic, disciplined approach to evaluate and improve the effectiveness of risk management, control, and governance processes."

Institute of Internal Auditors, June 1999

Audit in the e-context means looking at corporate operations and optimizing them for use of the e-operations being built by the new technologies.

Hence this means looking at companies and business with a view to assessing the organizational models required for e-business and assessing them accordingly.

Consider the following audit manager job description – the mission objectives in this auditing job description naturally lend themselves to extending observations into an e-context:

AUDIT MANAGER

Reporting directly to the President/Chief Executive Officer, your responsibilities will include:

» managing the Internal Audit Department including developing and implementing a co-sourcing internal audit process;
» applying comprehensive audit programs with a company-wide scope that will independently and objectively evaluate, advise,

and inform management on sufficiency of, and adherence to, corporate policies, procedures controls, and plans and compliance with government laws and regulations;

» preparing risk-based short- and long-term audit plans and programs;

» developing and implementing an internal audit value measurement system; and

» developing a strong working relationship with the Company's management, staff, external auditors, and regulators.

This job description illustrates the main concepts relating to the subject of audit and internal control.

NEW CONCEPTS

The Institute of Internal Auditors' definition of internal auditing quoted above reflects the way internal auditing is being practiced around the world today. It reflects the changes in terminology and the inclusion of several words or phrases such as "assurance," "consulting," "risk management," and "governance."

The inclusion of "assurance" and "consulting" reflects the broadened practice of today's internal auditing. The concept of "assurance services" is broader than the previous term "appraisal;" it does not obviate "appraisal," but it does recognize that there are other ways for internal auditing to provide service to the organization – and it allows internal auditing to use the same terminology that external auditors are beginning to market.

With respect to "consulting," many internal auditors have been able to respond to organizational challenges to add value through consulting or advisory activities without impairing the value of traditional audit services. Accordingly, practice today has expanded to incorporate a wide spectrum of assurance and consulting services not well described in the term "appraisal."

Internal auditing has always included assessing internal control in its scope, and there is no lessening today of this responsibility. Rather, the new definition recognizes that corporate governance has taken on added significance in many areas of the world and that controls exist to help manage risk.

By recognizing these factors in the definition, internal auditing is given the visibility to be a critical resource to the audit committee and senior management. Indeed, a key to promoting the profession is demonstrating to various stakeholders that internal auditors are equipped to provide quality service by *aiding management in the identification of risks* and providing assurance about the *effectiveness of the control structure*.

SUMMARY

As businesses evolve increasingly towards the structure of the e-corporation, the scope of audit and internal control will correspondingly evolve towards these new technologies.

Indeed, it is highly probable that the auditing and internal control profession will blend into a pool of IT and Internet-related competencies, yielding a new specialized subvariant of the auditing profession – that of e-audit and measurement: the ability to identify risks, define structures, and monitor the performance of e-enabled businesses.

Likewise, the impact of e-technologies in themselves promises to impact and enhance the effectiveness of the auditing and internal control function by facilitating dialogue and the exchange of information.

In this book, we also look at the implementation of audit directives and procedures on both sides of the Atlantic – measures recommended by the Office of the Comptroller of the Currency in the USA as well as initiatives being implemented by the EU Directorate in Europe. We also look at the implementation of frameworks to monitor derivatives activities in banks, and manage the risks arising from this activity.

The implementation of quality control initiatives such as ISO 9000 is also paramount in that they are closely linked to the audit and measurement role and offer a blueprint for achieving quality control throughout the organization.

Finally, we consider the role of audit and internal control and measurement as a discipline to enhance corporate performance, quality control, and effectiveness rather than as a dreaded tool used to "impose order from above."

Internal audit and measurement provides organizations with the tools to more effectively manage their operations and achieve excellence through quality control.

What is Internal Audit, Measurement, and Control?

» What is internal control?
» Everyday examples.
» Features of companies with strong internal controls.

Audits are concerned with a multiplicity of corporate operations – there are financial audits where the focus is on financial statements and the accuracy of the information contained therein. There are also other types of audits – compliance audits, performance audits, operational audits, etc.

The main issue here is that the term audit is larger than that typically understood by a financial audit.

"Internal audit and measurement," in the context of this work and e-series, relates to assessing organizational structures and performance. "Internal control" relates to the formation of structures and standards to implement corporate strategy and objectives, and the tools used to measure the performance of those systems.

Concomitant with internal audit and measurement is internal control.

WHAT IS INTERNAL CONTROL?

Internal controls are processes that provide reasonable assurance regarding the achievement of objectives in the following categories:

» effectiveness and efficiency of operations (i.e. are they functioning as intended?);
» reliability, accuracy, and timing of financial reporting; and
» compliance with applicable laws and regulations.

The principles of internal control can basically be illustrated by using common tasks in carrying out job responsibilities. Internal control is anything that you do to safeguard company assets or ensure the efficient and effective use of these assets. Internal controls help the company achieve its objectives.

On a day to day level, there are things you do every day without thinking of them as "internal controls." Some examples of these are:

» locking your desk and your office when you are not there;
» keeping your computer passwords secret;
» verifying the accuracy of another staff member's work;
» reviewing monthly department financial reports;
» depositing cash receipts daily;
» segregation of duties; and

» policies and procedures that are communicated and establish what should be done by whom.

The administrator who is responsible for the accomplishment of goals and objectives is also responsible for establishing, maintaining, and monitoring a good internal control system in a department. But every staff member should be responsible for assuring that established internal controls are followed and applied.

Internal control is important because when internal controls are weak, the company is more susceptible to inefficiencies such as:

» waste of company assets;
» inefficient procurement;
» inaccurate or incomplete information;
» misuse of company assets; and
» embezzlement and theft.

Companies with strong internal controls will exhibit the following features.

» Duties are divided among different people. For example, the same person does not initiate and approve a purchase and receive the goods.
» Authority limits are clearly defined in writing and communicated throughout the department.
» Accounts are reconciled on a timely basis.
» Equipment, supplies, inventory, cash, and other assets are physically secured and periodically counted and compared to records.
» Department policies are documented and reviewed periodically for current processes. In addition, policies are effectively communicated to all department staff.

To summarize:

» Internal audit enables a diagnostic examination to be made of the internal operations and workings of an organization, in particular identifying weak points in control structures which can lead to corporate downfall as illustrated by the Barings debacle or, more recently, by the financial shenanigans of Enron Corp., the natural gas conglomerate in the USA.

» Internal control offers the tools to implement the requisite structures to enable organizations to be effectively managed and controlled, as well as to implement the relevant reporting mechanisms required to enable management to reach effective and informed management decisions.

» Quality control initiatives such as the ISO 9000 program enable a consistency in the manufacturing (or service) process to be managed over successive time periods.

Together, these tools offer organizations the means to diagnose, manage, and ensure appropriate quality control throughout the organization.

Evolution of Internal Audit and Measurement

» Effective audit and internal control programs.
» The OCC and audits.
» Primary objectives of audits.
» Banks warned to protect Internet addresses.

The importance of audits has been demonstrated over time in uncovering anomalies and indeed often forms the focus of government initiatives and studies.

While internal audit and management forms a vast field of activity and professional orientation, in this work we will be looking at audit and internal control as it relates to the onset of the e-activated company and the implementation of appropriate structures.

Often, initiatives in this domain are stimulated by the government or regulatory agencies' pronouncements (which in turn are stimulated by industry developments such as the real-estate bubble in France, the debacle of derivatives trading on Barings in the UK, or the collapse and government bailout of the savings and loan industry in the USA). These developments translate into government/regulatory agencies' dictates in an effort to control adverse effects which are usually resolved at the taxpayer's expense. These various pronouncements in turn are implemented by auditors and companies into effective audit and internal control programs.

The end result is that the methodologies remain broadly similar in their systematic nature but the specificities are constantly affected by regulatory pronouncements and are in a constant state of evolution.

In the following section, we look at the viewpoint of the USA's Office of the Comptroller of the Currency on the state of the banking system and the role of audit and internal control and measurement on banks.

EFFECTIVE AUDIT AND INTERNAL CONTROL PROGRAMS

In the USA, the Office of the Comptroller of the Currency (OCC) has emphasized the importance of audit and internal control programs, in the light of recent examinations that have found deficiencies at many banks. For bank failures in the USA typically result in government bailouts, whatever the reason, due to the FDIC régime of the bank deposit guarantee scheme.

Effective programs were said to be necessary to:

» safeguard assets;
» assist in the timely detection of operational errors; and
» produce accurate bank records and financial reports.

According to the agency, some of the recently found problems have "caused significant operating losses and led to bank failures."

"The OCC is making effective internal controls in banks one of its top priorities in 2000," Comptroller John D. Hawke Jr said. Although banks were said to be in excellent condition, Hawke expressed concern that "continued pressure to maximize earnings can lead to a relaxation of internal control systems."

The OCC and audits

In its recent handbook, *The Internal and External Audits*, the OCC emphasizes the need for banks to establish and maintain strong internal control systems.

The handbook, distributed on July 24, 2000 to national banks and bank examiners, notes that effective internal and external audit programs are a critical defense against fraud and provide information to the board of directors about the effectiveness of internal control systems.

"A well-designed and executed audit program has always been an essential component of effective risk management, and is becoming ever more so as banking expands into new products, services, and technologies," said the OCC in a cover letter accompanying the handbook. "History offers many examples of serious problems that could have been avoided or identified earlier and mitigated, through proper audits."

Primary objectives of audits

According to the OCC, the primary objectives of internal audits are to independently and objectively:

» evaluate accounting, operating, and administrative controls;
» ensure that internal control systems result in accurate recording of transactions and proper safeguarding of assets; and
» determine whether the bank is complying with laws and regulations and adhering to bank policies.

The primary objectives of external audits are to provide the board of directors and management with:

» reasonable assurance about the effectiveness of internal controls over financial reporting, the accuracy and timeliness in recording transactions, and the accuracy and completeness of financial and regulatory reports;

» an independent, objective view of the bank's activities; and
» information useful in maintaining a bank's risk management processes.

Banks warned to protect Internet addresses

The OCC has also expressed concern over the safety of Internet addresses. According to the agency, national banks should select and protect their Internet addresses carefully.

Similarity in Internet addresses recently has caused some bank customers to erroneously transmit confidential information to the wrong Websites, according to the OCC.

The OCC recommends that banks should be certain that their Internet address – or domain name – is properly registered and under their control.

They also should consider registering any other "similar" domain names in order to protect customers from confusion. If a possibility of confusion with an existing Internet address exists, banks should consider using more intensive customer education, changing their domain name, acquiring the similar name, or using the available processes to dispute the similar name.

The E-Dimension

» Audit and internal control meets e-business.
» Information technology auditing.
» Internet as information source.

"The Road to Wisdom? Well, it's plain and simple to express: Err and err and err again but less and less and less."

Piet Hein[1]

AUDIT AND INTERNAL CONTROL MEETS E-BUSINESS

Auditing through the Internet leads to international connections – the Internet as a tool in the audit process has led to improved success of audits. The successes achieved were significantly influenced by incorporating the Internet as a research and information gathering tool as well as a communications tool.

The Internet has enabled auditors to consult the world pool of expertise (e.g. other auditors), enhancing the quality of their audit reports and proving that "internal audit" can and does "add value" to the organization. The dialogue potential offered by discussion forums also leads to auditors being able to offer tangible recommendations with a track record of success rather than hypothetical recommendations offered in isolation, thereby rendering the recommendations more convincing for senior managers considering implementation of the recommendations. Auditors offering proven recommendations can point to quantifiable data to support their recommendations.

The Internet is primarily used during the pre-audit research, best practice research, and reporting phases of audit processes.

We consider these phases below.

Pre-audit research

The pre-audit research phase uses the Internet in various ways.

Archive searches can be conducted on the various LISTSERV-based discussion groups specializing in auditing. Such lists can be either Internet discussion groups on Usenet, or LISTSERV-based e-mail-based discussion groups (e.g. majordomo *et al.*) such as Audit-L, Aaudit-L, IntAudit-L, and ACUA-L.

Instructions on how to sign up for LISTSERVs can be obtained from Patrick Douglas Crispen's Internet Roadmap Website http://netsquirrel.com/roadmap96/.

LISTSERV lists give you a way to have open discussions with dozens (or even hundreds) of people on a myriad of topics. Best of all, it is all done through e-mail!

Requests for information can be sent to "audit" discussion lists, and, for example, other "HR" discussion lists identified. This in effect represents a considerable pooling of audit intelligence and can lead to more effective and creative audit processes.

Information gained during this phase was also used during the strategic analysis phase of the audit process.

Best practice survey

A best practice survey focusing on the issues selected can be undertaken in consultation with the client. The survey can then be dispatched to hundreds of auditors via the audit discussion lists, and also to organizations and individuals identified during the pre-audit research phase.

In addition, specific segments of the survey can be sent to targeted "specialist" discussion lists. For example, in one audit, the training and development questions were sent to an Australian discussion list serving staff development specialists; whilst HR management information systems questions were targeted at a closed list of IT practitioners tackling the same issues in Canada.

Responses to the survey not only provide invaluable benchmarks, but also a range of options/solutions to problems encountered during the audit's detailed testing. The major advantage of these options was that they were practical solutions successfully applied in other organizations.

All survey responses were summarized and made available to participants.

Reporting

Audit discussion lists are useful when findings of the audit process need practical and appropriate recommendations, as numerous suggestions, advice, and offers of help will be posted.

These proven solutions involve less risk and are much easier to sell to management as viable alternatives to "doing nothing."

INFORMATION TECHNOLOGY AUDITING

Information Technology (IT) auditing has been accepted as a distinct profession carved out of two distinctly separate professions of IT-based data communications and auditing.

It is particularly relevant to the rise of e-business and e-operations. The standards adopted by the IT auditing profession are a blend of both of these.

We shall describe some of the activity-based standards borrowed from the erstwhile mainframe world and assimilated in IT audit activities and, in particular, those generally accepted by the practitioners of this profession. The attention is focused on the standards within an organization.

Standards

All the professional activities carried out by the IT department should be performed in a controlled and standardized manner. This is to ensure that the aims and objectives of the organization are complied with by the IT auditor or any professional connected to the IT department.

Often standards are unwritten and are generally accepted. This is counter-productive, because if the standards aren't documented, then there is no guarantee that everyone actually understands and follows them or that new employees are even aware of them.

IT auditors have accepted that standards need to be established, stabilized, and followed in the following areas of IT auditing with a specific reference to the system development life cycle.

System development life cycle (SDLC)

System development life cycle (SDLC) can possibly be considered a classical structure derived from the mainframe world. However, good practices from the mainframe world can be translated into today's client/server – or more complex – environment, and this is becoming more common.

The IT auditor needs to have a reasonable understanding of the environment and, more importantly, a practical approach to the work while reviewing the effectiveness of internal and external controls and the standards that the organization intends to follow.

There should be a set procedure, commonly known as the systems development life cycle, for the development of new systems.

Generally, the SDLC stages and required procedural standards are as follows.

» *Feasibility study*: The overall project feasibility is examined at this stage. A report is required to be issued and a review to ascertain whether the project should be continued. Various levels of authorization need to be specified, and this authorization should normally be by management which is the user of the services.

» *System design*: The system is specified in outline and estimates of costs and times are made. Again, there should be a requirement for review at this stage, especially to consider the cost and time estimates to determine if the project is still feasible.

» *Detailed design*: The constituent programs and processing flow are specified. There are a variety of methods of doing this, ranging from the pencil and paper method of specifying systems to the use of sophisticated prototyping methods and the use of CASE (Computer-aided Software Engineering) tools. Prototyping is where a dummy system is built, which can be discussed and tried out by the user until satisfied that it is what is required. CASE tools use various automated methods to determine data structures and process flows from which the system can be generated (almost automatically). Whatever method is in operation, it should be consistently applied throughout the organization. If many methods are in use, there is a danger of total confusion and wasted effort if responsibility for a project changes mid-stream.

» *Programming*: The programs are written at this time. Again, there are many methods, from line by line coding to sophisticated code generation, which can be found in CASE tools. The method is not important, but standards and consistency are.

» *Systems testing*: The computer department must carry out this testing to ensure that the system functions as specified. This testing is important to ensure that a working system is handed over to the user for acceptance testing.

» *Acceptance testing*: This testing needs to be carried out to ensure that the system functions as the user actually wanted. With prototyping techniques, this stage becomes very much a formality, necessary to check the accuracy and completeness of processing. The screen layouts and output should already have been tested during the prototyping phase.

» *Data capture*: For new systems, base data must be entered. Time and human resources must be allowed for this.

» *Data conversion*: Where a replacement system is being implemented there may be a requirement to convert data formats. There must be an allowance for this process to ensure that it is done accurately and completely.

» *Implementation*: In this stage, the system is handed over to the user for live operation. There can also be a period of parallel running to ensure that the system operates as required.

IT auditors should be involved at all stages of this process to ensure that the procedures are being adhered to and to ensure that the system contains all the required controls. Their involvement is discussed later in this series. The main purpose of the audit review of standards is to ensure that they are in place and are adequate. The effectiveness of and adherence to these standards will also be reviewed at a later stage during the review of applications under development.

Technical standards in SDLC stages

» *Analysis and programming*: In addition to the procedural controls provided by the SDLC standards, technical standards are also needed for systems analysis and programming to ensure continuity in the design and to reduce the reliance on the writer of the system. However, standards should also ensure that bad practices, which could lead to error and inefficiency in the operation of computer systems, are not prevalent.

» *Data structures*: The world is quickly becoming data-oriented. Standardization for storing it and defining it is of paramount importance. It is no longer acceptable for a programmer to define file (or database) layouts or organizations. Programmers must define standards for the way in which they carry out their task so that the entire organization can ensure that data is interchangeable and portable. Such standards should include details of acceptable database organization, naming conventions, and the procedures necessary to define new data items.

» *Security*: More and more people are gaining access to data stored on computers. These people can be employed by the organization and access the data over the organization's own networks, or they can be external to the organization, gaining access through public networks. Security is therefore becoming more and more important, especially with regard to data security. Consequently, the security requirements defined in the corporate policy must be implemented in a standard manner.

   » Systems should be designed to allow access only to those individuals and programs that need access to that data.
   » Equipment must be protected against damage or destruction, whether accidental or deliberate.
   » To ensure the security of data, access rights (read, update, delete, etc.) must be defined for all staff according to the varying sensitivity of the data.
   » These security standards should take into account any legislative requirements such as the need to protect personal data or matters of privacy.

» *Data controls*: All programs and systems should contain mechanisms that will provide for control to be exercised over the data being processed. It is essential that control be exercised in a standard fashion. Standards need to be defined for the control mechanisms to be applied.

» *Documentation*: Many people think documentation is a waste of time as nobody ever reads it and it's nearly impossible to keep it up to date! This is possibly true. However, in the event that something goes wrong and an inexperienced person is the only one available to correct it, documentation is worth its weight in gold. There must therefore be some discipline applied within any computer installation to produce some form of documentation. This discipline can come, in part, from publishing required standards.

   All systems should be documented to assist the maintenance process and to educate the users of the system. All aspects of the operation of the computing facility should be documented to provide a readily accessible reference source for all relevant persons within the organization who require information. All documentation should be accurate, complete, and current.

» *End-user programming*: As computer departments expand into monolithic structures, which cannot deliver all user requirements on time, the users themselves have begun to develop their own computer systems. Most of the tools they use have given them the ability to update data, as well as extract and analyze it. There is danger in allowing such systems development outside the controlled environment of the systems development area. Such development needs to occur within a framework of rules:
  » rules governing how data can be manipulated;
  » rules governing the types of software used for end-user programming; and
  » rules regarding the uses of output from end-user programs.

INTERNET AS INFORMATION SOURCE

In addition to the use of the Internet as a discussion forum, as we discussed with USENET, the Internet also facilitates audit and internal control, as well as quality control initiatives such as ISO 9000, by offering auditors the ability to access Websites for pertinent information.

The impact of regulatory pronouncements, guidelines on corporate governance, or updates to ISO standards can all be immediately accessed during the scope of the audit process.

This ensures that auditors are able to access the most current and up-to-date information; crucial when undertaking activities in regulatory based activities which are subject to regulatory change. Some of the advantages in compiling a ''library'' of Internet addresses to be consulted during the audit process include:

» addressing reference documents and procedural guidelines;
» accessing updated legislation; and
» posting guidelines via corporate intranets and communications.

CONCLUSION

The Internet and the impact of e-technologies in general on audit and internal control are therefore significant in two distinct ways:

» they impact the audit process, in that audits need to become cognizant of the new structures and paradigms of the e-enabled company; and

» they offer a communications tool to auditors to exchange problems and ideas and access current up-to-date information, ensuring that all auditors have access to first-class, current information and can discuss problems and solutions rather than operate in isolation.

The audit and internal control profession hence becomes empowered as well as transformed by the onset of e-technology.

NOTE

1 Hein, P. (1966) *Grooks*. The MIT Press, Cambridge, MA.

The Global Dimension

» E-technologies.
» ISO 9000.
» International convergence and EU financial legislation.

Moving back and looking at things from a global perspective, the field of audit and internal control and measurement is being impacted by several cross-border tendencies, which we now look at in some detail.

With the increasing complexity in the structure of the modern corporation, and the new paradigms being thrown up by IT and the new e-business models, we can identify several key areas, all having an effect on the way audit and measurement functions are carried out.

E-TECHNOLOGIES

The impact of e-technologies on organizational structures can be defined as:

> "All which relates to the linking of business, finance, and banking via electronic means, encompassing information gathering, processing, retrieval, and transmission of data as well as the transmission, purchase, and selling of goods and services."

A case in point is the use of Customer Relationship Management techniques arising from the use of client driven (as opposed to accounting driven) relational databases. CRM can assist in providing a more bespoke and personalized service to clients, which in turn impacts on issues of marketing strategy and branding of products and services.

A prime example of this is the online bookstore Amazon.com. Technology has revolutionized the hitherto staid book industry and enabled the creation of the Amazon "brand," which is merely the fruit of IT and relational databases with savvy marketing.

"E-finance," in common with "new economy," "e-commerce," or "e-business," is at present in its infancy, only hinting at the future networks and services that will be on offer.

The mission of audit and measurement in new companies will obviously impact the methodologies used in creating and monitoring organizational structures.

One of the first obstacles in considering e-finance is a definition dilemma and, consequently, the lack of an explicit definition of what it encompasses.

Globalization and internationalization are accompanied by new opportunities and challenges, as well as costs, risks, and threats.

ISO 9000

ISO 9000 is sweeping the world. It is rapidly becoming the most important quality standard. Thousands of companies in over 100 countries have already adopted it, and many more are in the process of doing so. This is because ISO 9000 controls quality, saves money, and reassures customers. Competitors also use it.

ISO 9000 applies to all types of organizations. It doesn't matter what size they are or what they do. It can help both product- and service-oriented organizations achieve standards of quality that are recognized and respected throughout the world.

ISO 9000 is closely related to audit and internal control in that it helps by implementing rigorous structures and procedures, which bodes well for the audit and internal control/measurement function.

ISO 9000 also provides a competitive edge, in that any company or organization which is ISO 9000 certified offers added reassurance to potential customers as to the seriousness and effectiveness of its structure as well as its ability to deliver consistent quality over time.

ISO 9000 can therefore be a means for a company to enhance its reputation in the markets or for a young start-up company to demonstrates its credentials of quality control, effective management structures, and professionalism more rapidly than building market presence organically over time.

INTERNATIONAL CONVERGENCE AND EU FINANCIAL LEGISLATION

The European Commission is at the heart of consultations on the future regulation of financial conglomerates, i.e. financial groups that offer a range of financial services. The consultations aim to address the supervisory issues that arise from the blurring of distinctions between the activities of firms in each of the banking, securities, investment services, and insurance sectors.

The Financial Services Action Plan envisaged the adoption of a Proposal for a Directive on the prudential supervision of financial conglomerates, in order to implement the recommendations of the Joint Forum on Financial Conglomerates adopted in February 1999.

The Commission stresses that it is crucial that the objectives of separate supervisors to ensure the capital adequacy of the entities for which they have regulatory responsibility are not impaired as a result of the existence of cross-sectoral financial conglomerates. It believes that this requires measures to prevent situations in which the same capital is used simultaneously as a buffer against risk in two or more entities which are members of the same financial conglomerate ("double gearing") and where a parent issues debt and downstreams the proceeds as equity to its regulated subsidiaries ("excessive leveraging").

The Commission further believes that an adequate and effective regulatory approach for intra-group transactions and risk exposures should be built on the following three pillars:

» an internal management policy with effective internal control and management systems;
» reporting requirements to supervisors; and
» effective supervisory enforcement powers.

Such regulatory initiatives by the EU obviously mean that internal audit and control mechanisms will need to be set in place in order to ensure that organizations are properly managed and safeguarded against violations of these directives. Such international developments and pronouncements will obviously have an effect on the "mission" of audit and internal control as inputs arising from internationalization of the business as well as regulatory mechanisms used to regulate those businesses.

The State of the Art – Internal Control and Derivatives

» Internal control issues in derivatives usage.
» Overview of derivatives and their environment.
» Utilizing the COSO Framework.
» Applying the COSO Framework.
» Roles and responsibilities.
» What to do.

"It's pretty easy to make money in this derivatives business."
*Peter Baring, prior to the collapse of Barings due to
derivatives trading*

The main challenge facing audit and internal control and measurement is keeping abreast of industry and technological developments.

Many auditing models have been developed over time, and while the methodologies and systematic procedures are time tested, their application is constantly being tested by evolution.

This is why business is replete with stories of corporate failure. For every lesson learnt in a business failure and regulatory framework erected in order to avoid a repeat disaster, there will be a new business model developed aiming to circumvent these restrictions on business "freedoms."

Often, new risks will occur in relatively new or poorly understood areas.

We therefore consider state of the art developments in banking and finance, to illustrate the role of audit and internal control in managing these developments. The Committee of Sponsoring Organizations report has become a tool to assist in developing business control systems and assessing their effectiveness. Many of the principles are applicable to a wide range of financial instruments, including derivatives trading.

INTERNAL CONTROL ISSUES IN DERIVATIVES USAGE

Problems surrounding the use of derivatives in recent years often revolved around difficulty in understanding their risks and their use for risk management purposes. These problems highlight the need for management to develop internal control systems for derivative activities.

The Committee of Sponsoring Organizations (COSO) report released in 1992, *Internal Control – Integrated Framework*, is becoming a widely accepted basis for developing business control systems and assessing their effectiveness.

This information tool was developed to help end-users of derivative products establish, assess, and improve internal control systems using the COSO Framework. Many of the control considerations discussed are also applicable to financial instruments other than derivatives.

The COSO Framework can also be applied to risk management activities in banks, for example, involving the use of derivatives. It can be used to help management design control processes, especially by providing direction for formulation of risk management policies. It also provides insights that enable those charged with oversight responsibilities to constructively examine existing policies and procedures. This information is augmented by the following supplements.

» *Supplement 1–Formulating Policies Governing Derivatives Used for Risk Management*: Describes the process of developing a policy governing derivatives use in the context of the overall risk management policy of an entity. It recognizes that risk management policies encompass all aspects of control. It also recognizes the importance of establishing clear and carefully written policies to avoid confusion and miscommunication, and provides examples of various aspects of a risk management policy for derivatives. This supplement can be used as a reference to formalize such a policy.

» *Supplement 2–Illustrative Control Procedures Reference Tool*: Provides examples of controls over derivative activities associated with each of the five components of control specified in the COSO Framework. It can be used as a reference for establishing, assessing, and improving controls relating to derivative activities, and can be useful for selecting controls considered to be appropriate in particular circumstances.

Overview of derivatives and their environment

Derivatives are financial contracts that derive their value from the performance of underlying assets (such as a stock, bond, or physical commodity), interest or currency exchange rates, or a variety of indices (such as a composite stock index like the Standard & Poor's [S&P] 500).

Derivatives include a wide assortment of financial contracts, including swaps, futures, forwards, options, caps, floors, and collars, whose values are based on defined formulas that apply to notional amounts (hypothetical reference amounts). Derivatives can also include certain assets and liabilities whose value and cash flows are directly determined by an underlying instrument or index, such as collateralized mortgage obligations, interest-only and principal-only certificates, and structured notes.

Other types of derivatives include contracts traded on organized exchanges standardized by regulation, as well as contracts that are traded in unregulated over-the-counter (OTC) markets, including individually tailored contracts negotiated between two parties for a specific purpose.

Risks associated with derivatives include market, credit, and liquidity, as well as various other risks. In addition to these technical risks, there is the fundamental risk that the use of these products may not be consistent with entity-wide objectives. Derivative use is sometimes misunderstood because, depending on the type of instrument and its terms, an instrument may be used to increase, modify, or decrease risk. As contract features increase in complexity, the value and effectiveness of a derivative in achieving objectives may become more difficult to ascertain before such positions are closed out or settled for cash. Derivative products and activities must be well understood in order for control systems to provide adequate assurance that derivatives use will support achievement of entity-wide strategies and objectives.

Utilizing the COSO Framework

"Control Principles in Derivatives Management"

This document relates to derivatives of each of the five components of control specified in the COSO Framework (the control environment, risk assessment, control activities, information and communication, and monitoring), focusing primarily on derivatives that are used for risk management purposes. An environment that provides for appropriate control over derivative activities generally has certain characteristics.

» *The control environment* consists of the integrity, ethical values, and competence of the entity's personnel, as well as management's philosophy and operating style. An active and effective board of directors should provide oversight. It should recognize that the ''tone at the top'' and the attitude toward controlling risk affect the nature and extent of derivative activities. The board should review management's planned decisions regarding the appropriateness and effectiveness of derivative strategies and positions. For example, the board should probe for explanations of past results to determine that derivative activities are effective in accomplishing the objectives for which they were used.

The audit committee should work with internal and external auditors to oversee implementation of risk management policies, procedures, and limits. Senior management should recognize that its philosophy and operating style have a pervasive effect on an entity. For this reason, senior managers should understand their control responsibilities, authorize use of derivatives only after risks and expected benefits have been carefully analyzed, and clearly communicate objectives and expectations for derivative activities. Senior managers should make a conscious decision about the extent of authority over derivatives delegated to management. Management should have the competence needed to understand derivative activities. Employees involved in such activities should possess the necessary skills and experience. The training process should develop and improve specific skills relating to responsibilities and expectations about derivative activities.

» *Risk assessment* is the identification and analysis of risks relevant to achieving objectives that form a basis for determining how risks should be managed. From a risk management perspective, entity-wide objectives relating to the use of derivatives should be consistent with risk management objectives. Mechanisms should exist for the identification and assessment of business risks relevant to the entity's unique circumstances. Use of derivatives should be based on a careful assessment of such business risks. Management should clearly link benefits of and support for derivative use with entity-wide objectives.

Management also should obtain an understanding of personnel, management operating systems, valuation methodologies and assumptions, and documentation as a foundation for identifying and assessing the capability to manage risk exposures associated with derivative activities. Management should provide specific measurement criteria for achieving derivative activities objectives, such as value at risk. Risk analysis processes for derivative activities should include identifying risk, estimating its significance, and assessing the likelihood of its occurrence.

» *Control activities* are the policies and procedures to help ensure that management directives are carried out. Policies governing derivative use should be clearly defined and communicated throughout the organization. The risk management policy should include procedures for identifying, measuring, assessing, and limiting business risks as the foundation for using derivatives for risk management purposes. The risk management policy for derivatives should include consideration of the following:

  » controls relating to managerial oversight and responsibilities;
  » the nature and extent of derivative activities, including limitations on their use; and
  » reporting processes and operational controls.

  The policy should provide for monitoring exposures against limits, and for the timely and accurate transmission of positions to the risk measurement systems. It also should provide for evaluation of controls within management information systems, including the evaluation of resources provided to maintain the integrity of the risk measurement system.

» *Information and communication* focus on the nature and quality of information needed for effective control, the systems used to develop such information, and reports necessary to communicate it effectively. Communications should ensure that duties and control responsibilities relating to derivative activities are understood across the organization. Adequate systems for data capture, processing, settlement, and management reporting should exist so that derivative transactions are conducted in an orderly and efficient manner. Mechanisms should be in place to obtain and communicate relevant information covering derivative activities. Directors and senior management should obtain sufficient and timely information to monitor achievement of objectives and strategies for using derivative instruments.

» *Monitoring* is the component that assesses the quality and effectiveness of the system's performance over time. Control systems relating to derivative activities should be monitored to ensure the integrity of system-generated reports. The organizational structure should include an independent monitoring function over derivatives, providing senior management with an understanding of the risks of derivative activities, validating results, and assessing compliance with established policies.

Applying the COSO Framework

» *Control Principles in Derivatives Management*: This tool recognizes that the nature and extent of derivatives use are frequently found in the overall risk management processes of an organization. Such processes, as they relate to the use of derivatives for risk management purposes, should generally involve the following.
   » Understanding operations and entity-wide objectives.
   » Identifying, measuring, assessing, and modifying business risk.
   » Evaluating the use of derivatives to control market risk and linking use to entity-wide and activity-level objectives.
   » Defining risk management activities and terms relating to derivatives to provide a clear understanding of their intended use.
   » Assessing the appropriateness of specified activities and strategies relating to the use of derivatives.
   » Establishing procedures for obtaining and communicating information and analyzing and monitoring risk management activities and their results.

Management may consider evaluating the appropriateness of the risk management processes governing derivatives against each of the five components of control specified in the COSO Framework.

Policies that document the risk management processes and provide for the use of derivatives should be carefully constructed to recognize that risk management means different things to different people. Precise reasons for using derivatives are not always apparent, and risk relating to certain activities and uses may be interpreted differently. Since there are no standard definitions of what risk management activities entail, appropriate control means that entities must use very specific language to describe expectations for using derivatives for risk management purposes. Policies should identify objectives and expected results, clearly define terms and limits, and identify and classify activities and strategies that are permitted, prohibited, or require specific approval.

Roles and responsibilities

Informed, involved senior-level governance is needed to ensure that risk management systems are in place and functioning as anticipated. The board of directors, its audit committee, and senior management have roles that represent critical checks and balances in the overall risk management system.

» *Board responsibilities*: The board of directors is responsible for overseeing the business of the entity, including its policies for managing risk and using derivatives. Monitoring and other day-to-day operations of the entity, on the other hand, are the responsibility of senior management. The policy direction provided by the board is important in determining the nature and extent of the use of derivatives. The board of directors provides oversight, reviews and approves the broad objectives to be accomplished, and provides specific delegation of responsibility and authority. It typically authorizes and approves management's strategies, operating plans, and policies for accomplishing objectives. This approval helps to ensure that activity-level objectives are consistent with broad entity-level objectives.

   The board of directors and senior management should carefully consider the resources required to use derivatives effectively. They should ensure that policies require employment of competent professionals to carry out risk management activities and strategies in accordance with its risk management policy and that such policy defines when reliance on outside advisors is appropriate. Further, compensation policies should be structured in a way that avoids incentives for excessive risk taking. The board should make a conscious decision about the amount of discretion that managers have in using derivatives.

» *Audit committee responsibilities*: The audit committee should understand the scope of internal and external audit testing of compliance with approved risk management policies, procedures, and limits and become comfortable that such controls appear to be functioning as intended. The audit committee also should be alert to the risk that such controls could be circumvented.

» *CEO responsibilities*: The CEO has overall responsibility for formulating derivatives policy and generally should be assisted in developing the policy and monitoring compliance by senior management who are not part of the day-to-day or derivatives management process. Senior management should formulate and implement approved policies, controls, and limits to ensure that the risks of derivative activities and the manner in which they are conducted are in accordance with the board's authorization.

» *CFO responsibilities*: The CFO also should be active in formulating the entity's derivatives policy and overseeing its implementation.

» *Controller responsibilities*: The controller is responsible for establishing the appropriate accounting treatment for all derivative activities. The corporate controller's department, not the individual business unit, should develop and document the accounting policies for derivatives. The corporate controller's department or other appropriate department independent of the business unit should also take an active role in applying the policies by assuming responsibility for documenting, assessing, and measuring compliance with appropriate accounting criteria.

» *Business unit responsibilities*: The business unit is responsible for recommending, approving, and executing risk management strategies. Segregating transaction initiation by the business unit and transaction review by the corporate controller or other appropriate independent department help establish necessary control over adherence to the entity's derivative policies and objectives.

What to do

Actions that might be taken to better understand or apply the COSO Framework to derivatives will depend on the position and role of the parties involved. A board of directors, senior management, and others involved with derivatives may consider a number of actions, including:

» initiating a self-assessment of entity-wide control systems, directing attention specifically to areas of derivative operations that are of primary importance;

» fully integrating management of derivative activities into the enterprise's overall risk management system by developing and implementing a comprehensive risk management policy;

» ensuring that policy objectives specifying the use of derivatives are clearly articulated and documented; and

» requiring that any use of derivatives be clearly linked with entity-wide and activity-level objectives.

Derivatives will continue to be an important business tool for managing an entity's risk management activities. Their significance is expected to increase with the development of new products and techniques that refine and improve the ability to achieve risk management and other objectives. Adequate understanding of the nature and risks of derivatives is essential to using these tools prudently. Improved awareness of how specific instruments behave under varying market conditions can only produce better-informed management decision making. Effective control is critical to any well-managed derivative operation. Control systems serve as the infrastructure for accomplishing entity-wide objectives. Applying the COSO Framework can help ensure that the use of derivatives is carefully integrated into the overall organizational control system and that unforeseen and undesirable outcomes are minimized.

Internal Audit and Measurement Success Stories

» Management audits in the European context.
» Checklist for public financial control.
» Responsibility for management (internal) control.
» Internal audit:
  » the mandate of the internal auditor
  » what does the internal auditor look for?
  » the independence of the internal auditor
  » audit trail
  » types of controls – preventive, detective, and corrective.
» Preparing for an audit.
» Types of audits.
» How will the audit findings be reported?
» Key findings.

In this chapter, we look at the tangible steps taken by the European Union in the implementation of audit and internal control guidelines in Europe.

The primary item of interest here is the widely varying nature of audit regimes in the EU, and how efforts to harmonize and strengthen the structures and guidelines are being made in Europe.

We consider these developments in light of the pressures building up to implementing measures, as well as a detailed look at the checklists and measures required to implement new audit structures in the EU.

The main importance of these developments is that it stresses the importance of implementing homogeneous, universally accepted and effective measures throughout the Euro zone.

MANAGEMENT AUDITS IN THE EUROPEAN CONTEXT

If management (internal) control is defined as the establishment of internal controls in the form of systems and procedures to counter the perceived risk, it is clear that it will vary widely from country to country and will reflect administrative culture and tradition.

A system that works well in one country may not transplant successfully to another. The main test of a system is how effective it is on the ground.

Among the EU Member States we find two broad approaches.

» One, which is found mainly in the southern countries, is what might be called the "third party ex-ante approach." In France, a transaction passes from the authorizing officer (the official of the line ministry who is entitled to authorize the transaction) to the financial controller designated by the Ministry of Finance, who certifies the legality and regularity of the transaction, and finally to an accountant of the Public Accounting Department to execute the transaction. A somewhat similar approach is found in a number of candidate countries (e.g. in Romania), where transactions have to be authorized and executed by the Treasury Department in the Ministry of Finance.

» The alternative approach in EU Member States, found mainly in northern countries, puts the emphasis on the personal responsibility of the official authorizing expenditure (or program manager) and of the head of the line ministry. In the United Kingdom, for instance, the person authorized to incur the expenditure will pass the transaction to the accounts department of his ministry, which will check the legality and regularity of the transaction before executing it. This is in effect an ex-ante control, but it takes place within and on the responsibility of the line ministry. If it is subsequently discovered that the transaction was irregular, it is the Permanent Secretary, i.e. the top civil servant in the ministry, who is held personally responsible and must account to Parliament through its powerful Public Accounts Committee. Most of the candidate countries correspond to the "southern" rather than the "northern" model, but changes are under way in a number of candidate countries.

The first model is rather law-oriented (the main function is to ensure that transactions are compliant with the law, including the annual budget law), whereas the second model could be seen as more management-oriented.

It has to be understood that both models, or any intermediate solution, are closely related to the context of each country. The "northern model" is appropriate for countries where the distinction between political responsibility and administrative responsibility is clearly and strongly established and where the risk of political interference with the routine management is minimal. The "southern model" could be a necessity in such situations where this risk is not totally ruled out and where tradition or legal status of civil service is not sufficient to protect the official in charge against it.

CHECKLIST FOR PUBLIC FINANCIAL CONTROL

It is important to ask several very basic questions when assessing the financial control situation in a country. These questions should of course be followed up in more detail.

» Is there a coherent and comprehensive statutory base in place defining the systems, principles, and functioning of financial control, and covering management (internal) control and internal audit or equivalent?

» Are there relevant management (internal) control systems and procedures in place? The systems and procedures analyzed are: accounting, procurement, ex-ante control, revenue control, audit trail, and reporting.
» Is there a functionally independent internal audit/inspectorate mechanism in place, with relevant remit and scope?
» Are there systems in place to prevent and take action against irregularities and to recover amounts lost as a result of irregularity or negligence?

RESPONSIBILITY FOR MANAGEMENT (INTERNAL) CONTROL

Following criticism by the European Parliament of financial management in the European Commission which led to the resignation of the entire Commission in March 1999, a committee of independent experts concluded that:

> "the existence of a procedure whereby all transactions must receive the explicit prior approval of a separate financial control service has been a major factor in relieving Commission managers of a sense of personal responsibility for the operations they authorize while [...] doing little or nothing to prevent serious irregularities..."

The committee recommended that a professional and independent Internal Audit Service should be set up reporting directly to the President of the Commission, that the existing centralized pre-audit function should be dispensed with, and that internal control – as an integrated part of line management – should be decentralized to the directorate-general.

In general the term "management (or internal) control" describes the systems, processes, and methods of organizing activities rather than a specific unit in the organization.

It is interesting to note, however, that the committee of independent experts reporting on the European Commission recommended a specialized internal control function exercised under the responsibility of a senior official reporting to the Director-General and an accounting function exercised under the responsibility of a delegated accounting officer.

INTERNAL AUDIT

Internal audit is a concept which flows logically from management (internal) control. In the EU context three internal audit models can be identified corresponding to the management (internal) control approaches previously referred to. In some of the candidate countries one can identify in addition what might be called the "control office" model or mentality (see below). There is no fixed ratio of internal audit staff to the financial and other resources audited and much depends on the extent to which systems audit techniques are used efficiently. The number of internal audit staff can vary from approximately 1000 in a large member state to about 100 in a small- or medium-sized administration.

Portugal is an example of the "southern" internal audit model. It has the Inspectorate-General for Finance (IGF) which depends directly on the Minister of Finance and is responsible for financial control of all public expenditure and revenue. In addition to the audit work carried out by the IGF there are internal audit units in the line ministries. Luxembourg has also adapted its "southern model" IGF system to incorporate internal audit procedures.

By contrast, the UK internal audit service in the Ministry of Finance is not responsible for "financial control of all public expenditure and revenue" but for ensuring that management control systems in the line ministries are such as to ensure effective financial control.

The Netherlands has a classical "northern model" system, with line ministries responsible for management (internal) control and reporting annually to Parliament. The internal auditors are co-ordinated by the Ministry of Finance and carry out mainly financial audits. They take account of the work of internal auditors at regional and municipality level and the external auditor receives and uses their reports.

The European Commission introduced the internal audit function in 1990 by creating a special service in the existing Directorate-General for Financial Control, which was a financial control service on the lines of the French system. The European Commission's internal audit service was given the mandate to carry out a financial audit in each Directorate-General every three to five years.

The audit examines the budgetary and financial systems and carries out substantive tests on a sample of transactions. It then establishes its conclusions as to the strengths and weaknesses of the systems and makes recommendations for any necessary improvements. A follow-up audit is carried out 12 to 18 months later.

In addition to financial audits, the internal audit service has been developing a performance audit capacity, and has increasingly been called upon to investigate problem areas and has identified substantial amounts for recovery.

Most candidate countries have no internal audit as such, but some have a "control office" or "control corps" based on the practice of the pre-1989 regime, which investigates complaints against staff from the public and may also investigate allegations of irregularity and fraud before turning the cases over to the criminal or fiscal police. Such units do not appear to audit financial management on any systematic basis.

The mandate of the internal auditor

The Institute of Internal Auditors defines internal audit as follows:

> "Internal auditing is an independent, objective, assurance and consulting activity designed to add value and improve an organization's operations. It helps an organization accomplish its objectives by bringing a systematic, disciplined approach to evaluate and improve effectiveness of risk management, control, and governance processes."

The internal audit does this by looking into how a selection of the transactions have been processed but also, and primarily, by assessing how the systems and procedures that build up the management (internal) control function. In practice the internal audit should cover two main types of audits – financial audit and performance audit.

» *Financial audit*: Audit of budgetary and financial systems with compliance tests ("walk-through" and substantive tests of actual transactions). Financial audits are generally carried out on the basis of an annual plan providing for each department to be covered at least once in the course of a multi-annual cycle. It may also involve a specific assessment of the effectiveness of accounting systems, including IT system safeguards and reporting facilities.

» *Performance audit*: Performance, or ''value-for-money'' audits, which should also be part of an annual plan, cover the extent to which established objectives and specific programs of the ministry or agency have been achieved or implemented, taking into account the extent to which they have been achieved – or not achieved – at a cost commensurate with the risk, and in an accurate and timely fashion with minimal use of resources.

Internal audit may also cover a specific analysis of staff resources with a judgement on the extent to which they correspond to the objectives of the ministry or agency and the tasks it is required to carry out.

What does the internal auditor look for?

The first concern of the internal auditor is that systems and procedures are in place to ensure that resources are used in accordance with the relevant rules and regulations.

This will often involve, particularly in the EU context, a requirement that an adequate sample of transactions or products is being checked by the national authorities.

For agricultural expenditure the auditor will wish to have solid evidence that grants to aid livestock or crop production have been used for that purpose, and that they have gone to farmers eligible for them.

Similarly, grants for training the unemployed must be shown to have been used for professional and effective training courses and for real and eligible applicants.

In the specifically EU context, a common problem found by the auditor is that funds are claimed for estimated expenditure, rather than for expenditure which has actually been incurred and paid.

In the area of public procurement the internal auditor will seek assurance that there has been adequate publicity for calls for tender, that there are satisfactory procedures for receiving and evaluating tenders, and that the justification for the award of contract is in accordance with national and/or EU requirements.

A Commission study in the late 1980s suggested that the European taxpayer would have paid more than €20bn less each year if public procurement throughout the Community had been in accordance with EU directives.

Overall, the internal auditor will look for evidence that both the program and any actions have achieved their objectives.

The independence of the internal auditor

The internal auditor should be responsible to the Minister or head of a ministry or agency, giving technical advice on the efficient management of resources without becoming involved in political questions.

In "southern model" countries the independence of the Inspectorate-General of Finance is assured by its reporting directly to the Minister of Finance. In "northern model" countries the internal auditor reports directly to the head (top official) of the ministry or agency. Practice varies in the candidate countries.

It is important to be clear about the nature of the internal auditor's independence. The Institute of Internal Auditors defines independence in the following terms:

> "Internal auditors are independent when they can carry out their work freely and objectively. Independence permits internal auditors to render the impartial and unbiased judgements essential to the proper conduct of audits. It is achieved through organizational status and objectivity."

It goes without saying that, as the Institute of Internal Auditors stresses, "internal auditors should be independent of the activities they audit."

Since the internal auditor is not independent of the ministry or agency in which he functions, it is essential for the internal audit function to achieve an appropriate status and weight in the organization.

One of the means of reinforcing the status of internal audit is to have an audit committee with, preferably, the head of the ministry or agency in the chair and representatives of senior management in addition to financial management and audit specialists.

The private sector as well as the public sector has come to recognize the value of the audit committee in ensuring that all levels of staff take internal audit seriously and give their full co-operation to the auditors.

The development of such attitudes on the part of the staff will help create the right conditions for effective management control.

An important function of an audit committee is to identify the areas to be covered by the audit program and the conclusions to be drawn from ongoing audits.

Audit trail

The auditor will almost always need an audit trail in one form or another.

In the national context it will be necessary:

» to trace the budget provision authorizing payment;
» to check the transfer of funds authorized by the Ministry of Finance (Treasury) to the line ministry and/or to the regional or local office;
» to trace and evaluate the systems/procedures through which approval for payment to contractor or beneficiary will be required to pass; and
» to locate completed payment files with evidence that payment has – or has not – been made in accordance with rules and regulations.

In the EU context it will be necessary:

» to identify the EU budget provision authorizing funding;
» to locate the flow of funds from the European Commission to the Ministry of Finance;
» to trace the flow of funds to the line ministry responsible for administering funding and identify procedures for registering arrival and onward movement of funds;
» to trace the flow of funds through regional and local offices and check procedures for registering arrival of funds, and the availability of national co-financing where appropriate, and identifying programs and projects for which they are intended, ensuring that EU and national funds are available for payment to the fund beneficiary on production of the appropriate proofs of expenditure and work or service completed;
» to trace the reverse flow of proof of eligible expenditure back through local and regional offices to the ministry responsible for administering funding; and

» to reconcile the proof of eligible expenditure for one or a series of projects with funds initially received and with the report back to the Commission.

Examination of the audit trail can be helpful to both the Commission and the Member State in identifying possible delays in the flow of funds and the implementation of projects, and possible difficulties in identifying items of expenditure and in reconciling the actual use of funds with the amounts initially transferred. It can also highlight weaknesses or gaps in the control procedures.

Types of controls – preventive, detective, and corrective

Controls can be designed for various functions. Some controls can be installed to prevent undesirable outcomes before they happen (preventive controls). Other controls can be installed to identify the undesirable outcomes when they do happen (detective controls). Still other controls can be installed to make sure that corrective action is taken to reverse undesirable outcomes or to see that they do not recur (corrective controls). All of these types of controls, in concert, function to ensure that some objective or goal will be met.

» *Preventive controls* are more cost-effective than detective controls and are designed to discourage errors and irregularities from occurring. When built into a process, preventive controls forestall errors and thereby avoid the cost of correction. Examples of preventive controls include:
  » trustworthy, competent staff;
  » segregation of duties to prevent intentional wrongdoing;
  » proper authorization to prevent improper use of resources;
  » adequate documentation and records as well as proper record-keeping procedures to deter improper transactions; and
  » physical control over cash, equipment, and other assets to prevent their improper conversion or use.
» *Detective controls* are usually more expensive than preventive controls, but are also essential, and are designed to find errors or irregularities after they have occurred. Detective controls measure the effectiveness of preventive controls. Also, some errors cannot

be effectively controlled through a system of prevention; they must be detected when they occur. Examples include: reviewing procurement card statements and phone charges for appropriateness, allowability, and/or proper allocation. Detective controls also include such control devices as bank reconciliations, independent checks on performance, confirmation of bank balances, cash counts, and systems of review like internal auditing.

» *Corrective controls* come into play when improper outcomes occur and are detected. All the detective controls in the world are valueless if the identified deficiency remains uncorrected or is permitted to recur. Corrective controls such as documentation and reporting systems keep problems under management surveillance until they have been solved or the defect corrected. Corrective controls thus close the loop that starts with prevention and passes through detection to correction.

PREPARING FOR AN AUDIT

Typically, department management will be notified in writing when it has been selected for an audit. This letter should state the objectives to be accomplished in the audit.

Subsequently, the Internal Audit Department will contact you to schedule a meeting to discuss the scope of the audit and the logistics of conducting the audit. At this initial meeting, you should take the opportunity to discuss any concerns or questions you may have about the audit, and to determine how you can facilitate the review process.

A typical audit has several stages, including preliminary research, data collection and analysis, review, report writing and distribution, and follow-up.

Generally the following process will occur once a unit is selected for review.

Audit planning

During this phase your unit will not be affected and may not even be aware it is occurring. The auditor assigned to the audit will review the files of prior audits in your area (if any), review applicable professional literature, research any applicable policies or statutes, and finally prepare an audit program, which is basically a list of steps to be performed on the audit.

Entrance conference

This is a meeting between the managers of the area being audited and personnel from Internal Auditing. This meeting introduces you to what will occur on the audit and allows you the opportunity to share any concerns you have. For example, if there is a particular process or procedure in your unit you would like us to review, let us know at this meeting and we can include it in our audit.

Fieldwork

During this process the auditor will test paper and/or electronic documents such as vouchers, reports, system files, and other departmental reports. The auditor will likely interview employees in the department to inquire about their duties and department process. We may flowchart the process we are reviewing to better understand the controls in place. Some of this work will be performed in our office and some in the unit being audited.

Report writing

Throughout our review we will attempt to be open regarding what we find and plan to recommend in our report. Once we've completed our fieldwork, the auditor in charge will write a report which states what we did, what we found, and any recommendations for improvement. After this report is completed, a rough draft will be given to the department manager for their review.

Exit conference

The exit conference is a meeting between departmental management and personnel from Internal Audit and Management Advisory Services (usually the same people that were in the entrance conference). This may occur in person, by phone, or e-mail. At this meeting we will together review the report and our findings. If we have misinterpreted anything in our report, this provides you with the opportunity to let us know before the report is seen by anyone else. It also allows us the opportunity to discuss our recommendations. Occasionally, we will make oral recommendations on items we don't include in the report. We will discuss any oral recommendations in this meeting.

Final audit report

After the exit conference, we will make any changes to the audit report agreed upon in the exit conference. Administrative responses/comments from the managers of the unit being audited will be inserted into the report. All levels of management involved with this audit will receive a copy of the final audit report. A summary of the report will be provided to senior management.

Disposition of recommendations

The Internal Audit department will contact you within one year after the audit report is issued to determine whether the recommendations have been implemented, and if not, why they have not been implemented. The follow-up report will be sent to senior management.

TYPES OF AUDITS

There are six general categories of internal audit reviews:

» *Internal control reviews* are the most limited form of audit performed. We will assess the adequacy of internal controls through completing questionnaires and flow charts. Limited audit testing will be performed.
» *Financial audits* address questions of accounting, recording, and reporting of financial transactions. Reviewing the adequacy of internal controls also falls within the scope of financial audits.
» *Compliance audits* seek to determine if departments are adhering to (for example) Federal, State, and MCCCD rules, regulations, policies, and procedures.
» *Operational audits* examine the use of resources to evaluate whether those resources are being utilized in the most efficient and effective way to fulfil the mission and objectives. An operational audit may include elements of a compliance audit, a financial audit, and an information systems audit.

» *Investigative audits* are performed when appropriate. These audits focus on alleged violations of federal and state laws and of MCCCD policies and regulations. This may result in prosecution or disciplinary action. Audits precipitated by internal theft, misuse of MCCCD assets, and conflicts of interest are examples of investigative audits.

» *Information systems (IS) audits* address the internal control environment of automated information processing systems and how these systems are used. IS audits typically evaluate system input, output and processing controls, backup and recovery plans, and system security, as well as computer facility reviews.

HOW WILL THE AUDIT FINDINGS BE REPORTED?

Audits can last from several days to several months. The auditor assigned to your unit should provide an estimate of the time needed to complete the audit.

You and your staff will be kept apprised of the auditor's findings throughout the course of the audit. At the conclusion of the audit, you will be able to review a draft of the report before the final version is issued. Typically, the auditor will maintain the confidentiality of sources and audit information until the report is issued. The final report is a ''public'' document.

KEY FINDINGS

In any effective audit process, it is crucial that a systematic approach be adopted, based on established methodologies and procedures. However, this should not obscure the fact that every organization is different and involved in different activities. Hence, the effectiveness of the audit will be directly related to the fact that it will take into account the specificities of the situation. This requires rigorousness in adhering to established methodologies and guidelines but also the ability to think ''outside the box'' in focussing on the specificities of the organization, as well as the impact of new technologies on the business models and new organizational structures of the e-enabled company.

Key Concepts and Thinkers

» ISO 9000 and building the audit ready company.
» Overview of the ISO 9000 family of publications.
» ISO 9000-1.
» ISO 9000-2.
» ISO 9000-3:1997(E).
» ISO 9000-4.
» Glossary.

The audit profession is not animated by key thinkers or gurus in the Warren Buffet or Donald Trump mould, as the profession does not benefit from a high profile glamour image.

However, there are key concepts and thinking going on in the industry. One of the main developments related to audit and internal control is the implementation of ISO 9000. ISO 9000 aims at defining and implementing organizational structures which adhere to quality management processes. Hence, ISO 9000 is closely related to audit and internal control in that it helps by implementing rigorous structures and procedures which bode well for the audit and internal control/measurement function.

ISO 9000 also provides a competitive edge, in that ISO 9000 certification provides added reassurance to potential customers as to the seriousness and effectiveness of an organization's structure, as well as its ability to deliver consistent quality over time.

ISO 9000 can therefore be a means for a company to enhance its reputation in the markets or for a young start-up company to demonstrate its credentials of quality control, effective management structures, and professionalism more rapidly than building market presence organically over time.

We therefore turn to an examination of ISO 9000 as it impacts organizational structures and behavior and as a key element in the creation of effective internal audit and measurement structures. In this chapter, we look at the concept and development of ISO 9000 as well as some of the methodologies and checklists to consider in obtaining ISO certification.

ISO 9000 AND BUILDING THE AUDIT READY COMPANY

ISO 9000 is sweeping the world. It is rapidly becoming the most important quality standard. Thousands of companies in over 100 countries have already adopted it, and many more are in the process of doing so. Why? Because it controls quality. It saves money. Customers expect it. And competitors use it.

ISO 9000 applies to all types of organizations. It doesn't matter what size they are or what they do. It can help both product and service oriented organizations achieve standards of quality that are recognized and respected throughout the world.

ISO is the International Organization for Standardization. It is located in Switzerland and was established in 1947 to develop common international standards in many areas. Its members come from over 120 national standards bodies.

What is ISO 9000?

The term ISO 9000 refers to a set of quality management standards. ISO 9000 currently includes three quality standards: ISO 9000:2000, ISO 9001:2000, and ISO 9004:2000. ISO 9001:2000 contains requirements, while ISO 9000:2000 and ISO 9004:2000 are guidelines. All of these are process standards (not product standards).

ISO first published its quality standards in 1987, revised them in 1994, and then republished an updated version in 2000. These new standards are referred to as the "ISO 9000 2000 Standards."

ISO's purpose is to facilitate international trade by providing a single set of standards that people everywhere can recognize and respect.

The ISO 9000 2000 Standards apply to all kinds of organizations in all kinds of areas: manufacturing, processing, servicing, electronics, steel, computing, legal services, financial services, accounting, pharmaceuticals, oil and gas, pulp and paper, petrochemicals, publishing, shipping, energy, telecommunications, aviation, software development, tourism, biotechnology, chemicals, engineering, farming, entertainment, consulting, insurance, and so on.

How does ISO 9000 work?

You decide that you need to develop a quality management system that meets the new ISO 9000 Standards. You choose to follow this path because you feel the need to control or improve the quality of your products and services, to reduce the costs associated with poor quality, or to become more competitive.

Alternatively, you choose this path simply because your customers expect you to do so or because a government body has made it mandatory.

You then develop a quality management system that meets the requirements specified by ISO 9001:2000.

How do you develop such a system?

The first step is to start with a Gap Analysis. An ISO 9001 2000 Gap Analysis will tell you exactly what you need to do to meet the new ISO 9001 2000 Quality Management Standard. It will help you identify the *gaps* that exist between the new ISO 9001 Standard and your organization's processes. Once you know precisely where the *gaps* are, you can take steps to fill your gaps.

By doing so, you will not only comply with the new ISO 9001 Standard, but you will also improve the overall performance of your organization's processes.

Once your quality system has been fully developed and implemented, you carry out an internal audit to ensure that you've met every single ISO 9001 2000 requirement.

When you're ready, you ask a registrar to audit the effectiveness of your quality management system. If your auditors like what they see, they will certify that your quality system has met ISO's requirements. They will then issue an official certificate to you and they will record your achievement in their registry.

You can then announce to the world that the quality of your products and services is managed, controlled, and assured by a registered ISO 9001 Quality Management System!

While you don't have to be registered, your customers are more likely to believe that you have an effective quality management system if an independent external auditor says so.

Why is ISO 9000 important?

ISO 9000 is important because of its international orientation. Currently, ISO 9000 is supported by national standards bodies from more than 120 countries. This makes it the logical choice for any organization that does business internationally and needs to meet international standards of quality.

ISO is also important because of its systemic orientation. This is crucial. Many people equate success with motivational and attitudinal factors. This is fine, but insufficient – unless you institutionalize the right attitude by supporting it with the right policies, procedures, records, technologies, resources, and structures, you will never achieve the standards of quality that other organizations seem to be able to achieve. Unless you establish a quality attitude by creating a quality system, you will never achieve a world-class standard of quality.

Simply put, if you want to have a quality attitude you must have a quality system. This is what ISO recognizes, and this is why ISO 9000 is important.

OVERVIEW OF THE ISO 9000 FAMILY OF PUBLICATIONS

ISO refers to ISO 9000-1 as a "road map" for the ISO family of publications. It provides a quick "tour" by briefly explaining what each ISO publication is about.

» Use ISO 9000-1 if you need to clarify concepts and to see which ISO publications you should study.
» Use ISO 9000-2 if you need some help implementing ISO 9001, ISO 9002, or ISO 9003.
» Use ISO 9000-3 if you are in the software business and you want to use ISO 9001 to set up a quality system.
» Use ISO 9000-4 if product dependability is important. Dependability means reliability, maintainability, and availability.
» Use ISO 9001 if you design, develop, produce, install, and service products, and if your customers need to be satisfied that product anomalies will be avoided via ISO 9001's Quality Assurance Model.
» Use ISO 9002 if you produce, install, and service products. ISO 9002 presents a Quality Assurance Model that will help you to develop the appropriate quality system.
» Use ISO 9003 if product quality can be assured through final inspection and testing. ISO 9003 presents a Quality Assurance Model that will help you to develop the appropriate quality system.
» Use ISO 9004-1 if you intend to develop a quality system. ISO 9004-1 lists the elements that make up a quality system.
» Use ISO 9004-2 if customer service is important to your organization. ISO 9004-2 discusses elements and concepts.
» Use ISO 9004-3 if your organization processes solids, liquids, or gases as part of your production process.
» Use ISO 9004-4 if you need to generate quality improvements. It discusses concepts and methods.

» Use ISO 10011-1 to develop your internal quality audit program. It explains how to verify the existence of quality elements and how to verify that your quality objectives are being met.
» Use ISO 10011-2 to develop your internal quality audit program. It describes the qualifications that your internal auditors should have.
» Use ISO 10011-3 to develop your internal quality audit program. It describes how a quality system audit program should be managed.
» Use ISO 10012-1 to ensure that your quality assurance measuring equipment meets all ISO requirements.

ISO 9000-1

ISO 9000-1 provides an introduction to the ISO 9000 family of publications, briefly explaining what each ISO publication is about. But it also discusses some concepts and makes some general theoretical points.

Requirements

ISO 9000-1 distinguishes between quality system requirements and product quality requirements.

» Quality system requirements are characteristics or properties that systemic elements should have.
» Product quality requirements are characteristics or properties that products (or services) should have.

ISO 9000-1 distinguishes between four types of products: hardware, software, processed materials, and services. Notice that a service is a product.

The quality of your product depends on:

» whether you routinely update it to meet changing market requirements and opportunities;
» whether you design into your product the characteristics the marketplace needs and wants;
» whether every instance of your product precisely conforms to your product design; and
» whether you provide customer support throughout the life cycle of your product.

All work is a process.

» Every process is a transformation.
» Every process has inputs and outputs.
» Every process transforms inputs into outputs.

An organization is a network of processes.

» Organizations must identify, organize, and manage this network of processes.
» The link or interface between each process must be clearly defined and well managed.

Product quality depends on how well this network of processes works, therefore:

» this network must be routinely monitored and analyzed; and
» the continuous improvement of this network must be a high priority.

A quality system is a network of processes.

» These processes must be well integrated and properly co-ordinated.
» The link or interface between each process must be clearly defined and well managed.

When evaluating a quality system process, you must ask:

» have you developed procedures to control this process?
» are the procedures that control this process both documented and well defined?
» are the procedures that define this process completely deployed and implemented? and
» are the procedures that define this process able to generate the necessary results?

Quality systems are evaluated by:

» executive managers;
» quality auditors; internal auditors; first party auditors; your employees;
» external auditors; second party auditors; your customers; and
» third party auditors; independent bodies.

A process is documented by writing procedures.

» Your quality system should be documented by writing procedures.
» If you document your current quality system procedures, changes in quality are easier to detect and to measure because they can be compared with the way things were done in the past.

Documents provide objective evidence that:

» a process has been defined;
» procedures have been approved; and
» procedural changes are under control.

ISO 9000 – 2

ISO prepared 9000–2 to help implement ISO 9001, ISO 9002, and ISO 9003. While ISO 9000-2, ISO 9001, ISO 9002, and ISO 9003 use the same numbering system to simplify cross-referencing, this similarity breaks down at the more detailed level.

Management responsibility

» Your senior managers must demonstrate their continuous commitment to your quality policy and your quality system. This commitment must be both active and visible.
» Make sure all management and staff members understand how their jobs affect quality.
» Encourage everyone in your organization to feel responsible for the quality of your products and services.
» Appoint people to monitor your quality system and to report their observations directly to senior management.
» Provide the resources that people need to verify quality work.
» Quality system reviews should be carried out by senior managers.
» Changes to the quality system must be implemented without delay.

Quality system

» Your quality manual could be several manuals. You could have one quality system manual that is supported by several more detailed procedure manuals. All of these define your quality system.

» Quality plans can also have several levels, from general to specific. Like procedures, quality plans explain how quality requirements will be met. But, unlike procedures, plans are usually tied to a time frame and often involve contractual obligations.

Contract review

» Make sure you understand what customers need.
» Make sure that everyone who must review contracts in fact does so.
» Make sure that all contract review concerns and questions are answered before the contract is finalized.

Design control

» Design control is very important because many quality requirements can be satisfied through good design.
» Make sure you develop plans to evaluate, test, and measure the safety, dependability, and performance of your products.
» Your design teams should know what kinds of information should be shared, who should get this information, how it should be transmitted, and what records should be kept.
» Use a "design description document" to record design agreements and solutions. And develop procedures to update and distribute this design description document.
» Use at least two different methods to verify your design outputs.
» Your design reviewers should be competent.
» Your designs should deal with safety and environmental issues.
» Your designs should meet functional and operational requirements.
» Make sure you can actually implement your design.
» Verify the accuracy of design calculations done by computer.
» Verify the validity of all your design assumptions.
» Test your products in realistic settings.
» When designs must be changed, after the design phase is finished, make sure that previous design verification results are still valid.
» When designs have been changed, make sure your design verification procedures are still valid.

Document control

» Control documents by maintaining a central registry that specifies exactly which documents should be controlled, their revision status, what kinds of approvals they need, and how they should be distributed and stored.

» Control documents and data in areas such as purchasing, design, and inspection. In general, all documents and data related to the quality system, and the work that is carried out within the system, should be controlled.

» Develop procedures that specify exactly which documents should be controlled and who should control them, as well as how, when, and where this control should occur.

» Develop procedures to control changes in documents and data.

Purchasing

» Make sure that you have a good working relationship with your subcontractors (suppliers), and make sure that the lines of communication and feedback are always open.

» Maintain records that show how each subcontractor is selected. Make sure that these records show that each subcontractor meets your quality and contract requirements.

» Review the performance of your subcontractors on a regular basis.

» Make sure that you specify who is responsible for reviewing and approving purchasing documents and data, including purchase orders and contracts.

Customer-supplied product

» Clarify who is responsible for telling the customer that products supplied to you by him are unsuitable.

» You (the supplier) should ensure that all products and services provided by your customers are suitable.

Product identification and tractability

» Mark or tag products, product batches, or product containers.

» You may need to use special identifiers to indicate:
  » who worked on the product;
  » what raw materials were used;
  » what tools and equipment were used; and
  » what process methods were applied.

» Inspection and stock records should use product identifiers.

Process control

» All products (and services) are created by means of processes.
» Process control is necessary to avoid product nonconformities.
» Control the process characteristics that influence product quality.
» Monitor and control the materials that enter your processes.
» Monitor and control the materials that are inside your processes.
» Develop procedures to ensure that:
  » process software and hardware works properly; and
  » process materials are suitable and properly stored.

Inspection and testing

» Develop procedures that explain how your staff should verify that incoming shipments meet all contractual requirements.
» Develop procedures that explain how your staff should handle incoming shipments that do not conform to requirements.
» When incoming shipments are subject to future recall, try not to release them for use until you have inspected them.
» Develop procedures to control what happens to incoming products that are released without inspection and later found not to conform.
» Clarify who has authority to release incoming products subject to recall and describe the conditions under which release is allowed.
» In-process inspection should be carried out in order to detect nonconformities as early as possible.

Inspection, measuring, and test equipment

» Your measurement process should ensure that:
  » appropriate measurements are done;
  » suitable measuring equipment is used; and
  » effective measuring procedures are applied.
» Measurement instruments can be either tangible (e.g. equipment) or intangible (e.g. questionnaires).

Inspection and test status

» The inspection and test status of your products should be clearly indicated by means of tags, marks, numbers, physical location, or any other suitable means.

» Your inspection and test procedure should identify and segregate products that:
  » have not been inspected; or
  » have been inspected and have either been:
    » accepted;
    » rejected; or
    » placed on hold.

Control of nonconforming products

» Develop procedures to prevent the inappropriate use of nonconforming products. These procedures should cover both your own products and the products supplied to you by your subcontractors (suppliers).
» Make sure that you identify exactly where each nonconforming product came from, when and how it was produced, and what caused the problem.

Corrective action

» Product nonconformities can be caused by:
  » tool and equipment faults and malfunctions;
  » material and supply defects and deficiencies;
  » systemic weaknesses and shortcomings;
  » process failures and deficiencies;
  » process control defects and breakdowns;
  » procedural gaps and weaknesses; or
  » human ignorance and negligence.
» Product nonconformities can be discovered by:
  » examining inspection, testing, and nonconformity documents;
  » observing work activities and processes;
  » conducting quality audits and reviews;
  » reviewing customer ideas and complaints;
  » analyzing regulatory input and observations; or
  » studying staff suggestions and feedback.

Handling, storing, packaging, and delivery

» Procedures for handling, storing, packaging, and delivery should cover both in-process materials and finished products.

» Tools and equipment, used to handle products, should be appropriate and well maintained.
» Storage methods should ensure that products are secure and protected from damaging environmental conditions.
» Packaging methods must ensure that products are identified and protected against damage, deterioration, or contamination.
» Delivery methods must ensure that products are protected from loss, damage, deterioration, or contamination.

Quality records

» Develop a record keeping system that can prove that your products meet requirements and your quality system is implemented. Your records can be either paper-based or electronic as long as they document the performance of your quality system.
» When you determine how long old quality system records should be kept, consider contractual and regulatory requirements as well as the life expectancy of your products.

Internal quality audits

» Periodic internal quality audits should be done to:
  » determine whether you have documented all quality elements;
  » determine whether you have implemented all quality elements;
  » evaluate how effective your quality system is;
  » improve your quality system; and
  » prepare for external quality audits.
» Special internal audits may also be done after major systemic or procedural changes have been made or after significant problems have been solved. This type of audit is done to verify that the changes were effective and that the problems really were solved.

Training

» Make sure that your training records keep track of the training provided and the results that were achieved.
» Training and awareness activities should be carried out in order to:
  » show people how to carry out tasks;
  » show people how to apply procedures; and
  » motivate people to support quality.

Servicing

» If your products require after-sale service or post-installation support, you should clarify how service responsibilities will be shared between you, your distributors, and your customers.
» Make sure that:
  » customers and distributors know how to service products;
  » service delivery people receive technical support;
  » service delivery people receive training;
  » you develop product service delivery plans;
  » your service and test equipment is effective;
  » you have an adequate supply of spare parts; and
  » you set up an information feedback system.

Statistical techniques

» Use statistical methods to help you:
  » decide what data to collect;
  » make the best use of your data;
  » control processes;
  » avoid nonconformities;
  » measure quality characteristics;
  » design products and services;
  » define product and process limits; and
  » identify problems and analyze causes.

ISO 9000 – 3:1997(E)

ISO prepared the 9000–3:1997(E) guidelines in order to help organizations to apply the ISO 9001 standard to computer software. Use ISO 9000–3 if you develop, supply, install, and maintain computer software.

Management responsibilities

» Define a quality policy. Your policy should describe your organization's attitude towards quality.
» Define the organizational structure that you will need in order to manage your quality system.
» Define quality system responsibilities, give quality system personnel the authority to carry out these responsibilities, and ensure that

the interactions between these personnel are clearly specified. Also, make sure that all of this is well documented.

» Identify and provide the resources that people will need to manage, perform, and verify quality system work.

» Appoint a senior executive to manage your quality system and give him or her the necessary authority.

» Define a procedure that your senior managers can use to review the effectiveness of your quality system.

Quality system requirements

» Develop and implement quality system procedures that are consistent with your quality policy.

» Develop quality plans which show how you intend to fulfil quality system requirements. You are expected to develop quality plans for products, processes, projects, and customer contracts.

» Develop quality plans to control software development projects.

» Develop a quality plan whenever you need to control the quality of a specific project, product, or contract.

» Your quality plan should explain how you intend to tailor your quality system so that it applies to your specific project, product, or contract.

» Develop detailed quality plans and procedures to control configuration management, product verification, product validation, nonconforming products, and corrective actions.

Contract review requirements

» Develop and document procedures to co-ordinate the review of sales orders and customer contracts. Make sure you include the customer in the process of review.

» Develop and document procedures to co-ordinate the review of software development contracts.

» Your contract review procedures should ensure that all contractual requirements are acceptable before you agree to provide products or services to your customers.

» Make sure that you and your software customer agree on:
  » how terms will be defined;
  » how products will be accepted;
  » how the customer will participate;

» how software users will be trained;
» how software upgrades will be handled;
» how joint progress reviews will be conducted;
» how changes in customer requirements will be handled; and
» how problems will be handled after product acceptance.
» Make sure that you and your customers agree that:
  » the project is feasible;
  » the legal rights of others will be respected; and
  » the customer can meet all contractual obligations.
» Make sure that you have:
  » established a project schedule;
  » identified significant risks and contingencies;
  » specified all contractual liabilities and penalties;
  » defined your software development procedures;
  » confirmed that resources will be available when needed; and
  » clarified the extent of your responsibility for subcontractors.
» Develop procedures which specify how customer contracts are amended, and which ensure that changes in contracts are communicated throughout the organization.
» Develop a record keeping system that you can use to document the review of customer orders and contracts.

Product design requirements

» Develop and document procedures to control the product design and development process. These procedures must ensure that all requirements are being met.
» Control your software development projects and make sure they are executed in a disciplined manner.
» Control your software design process and make sure that it is performed in a systematic way.
» Develop product design and development planning procedures.
» Prepare a software development plan. Your plan should be documented and approved before it is implemented. Your plan should:
  » define your project;
  » list project objectives;
  » present your project schedule;
  » define project inputs and outputs;

> » identify related plans and projects;
> » explain how your project will be organized;
> » discuss project risks and potential problems;
> » identify important project assumptions;
> » identify all relevant control strategies; and
> » identify the groups who should be routinely involved in the product design and development process, and ensure that their design input is properly documented, circulated, and reviewed.
» Make sure that your software development plan defines:
> » how the responsibility for software development will be distributed amongst all participants; and
> » how technical information will be shared and transmitted between all participants.
» Make sure that your customer has accepted the responsibility to co-operate and support your software development project.
» Make sure that you schedule project reviews in order to evaluate the activities and the results achieved by all participants.
» Develop procedures to ensure that all design input requirements are identified, documented, and reviewed; and that all design flaws, ambiguities, contradictions, and deficiencies are resolved.
» Design input requirements should be specified by the customer. However, sometimes the customer will expect you to develop the design-input specification. In this case you should:
> » prepare procedures that you can use to develop design-input specifications;
> » work closely with your customer in order to avoid misunderstandings and to ensure that the specification meets the customer's needs and expectations;
> » express your specification using terms that will make it easy to validate during product acceptance; and
> » ask your customer to approve the resulting design-input specification.
» Develop procedures to control design outputs.
> » Prepare design output documents using standardized methods and make sure that your documents are correct and complete.
> » Develop procedures which specify how product design reviews should be planned and performed.

» Plan and perform product design reviews for your software development projects.

» Develop and document software design review procedures.

» Develop procedures which specify how design outputs, at every stage of the product design and development process, should be verified.

» Verify your software design outputs by performing design reviews, demonstrations, and tests.

» Maintain a record of your design verifications.

» Develop procedures that validate the assumption that your newly designed products will meet customer needs.

» Prove that your product is ready for its intended use before you ask your customer to accept it.

» Accept validated products for subsequent use only if they have been verified and only if all remedial actions have been taken.

» Maintain a record of your design validations.

» Develop procedures to ensure that all product design modifications are documented, reviewed, and formally authorized before the resulting documents are circulated and the changes are implemented.

» Develop procedures to control software design changes that may occur during the product's life cycle.

Document and data control

» Develop procedures to control quality system documents and data.

» Identify all documents and data that must be controlled.

» Develop procedures to control your documents and data.

» Develop procedures to review, approve, and manage all of your quality system documents and data.

» Develop procedures to control electronic documents and data.

» Develop procedures to control changes to documents and data.

Purchasing requirements

» Develop procedures to ensure that purchased products meet all requirements. These procedures should control the selection of subcontractors, the use of purchasing data, and the verification of purchased products. The term purchased products includes both products and services.

» Develop procedures to select, evaluate, monitor, and control your subcontractors (your suppliers). Make sure that quality records are kept which chronicle the performance of all your subcontractors. Your records should identify the acceptable subcontractors and the products and services they provide.
» Develop procedures to ensure that your purchasing documents precisely describe what you want to buy.
» Develop procedures that allow you or your customers to verify the acceptability of products you have purchased.

Customer-supplied products
Develop procedures to control products supplied to you by customers. These procedures should ensure that you:

» examine the product when you receive it to confirm that the right items were shipped without loss or damage;
» prevent product loss, misuse, damage, or deterioration through proper storage and security;
» record, and report to the customer, any product loss, misuse, damage, or deterioration;
» clarify who is responsible for the maintenance and control of the product while it is in your possession; and
» control products, services, documents, and data supplied by customers.

Product identification and tracing
» Develop and document procedures to identify and track products from start to finish. When appropriate, these procedures should ensure that you:
  » identify and document products every step of the way from the purchase of supplies and materials through all stages of handling, storage, production, delivery, installation, and servicing;
  » trace products or product batches by means of unique identifiers and suitable record keeping;
  » develop procedures to assign unique identifiers to your software products and components; you should assign identifiers during the product definition phase and be able to maintain these identities throughout the product life cycle;

» develop procedures to track your software products and components; you should be able to track your software throughout its life cycle; and

» use configuration management methods to identify and track your software products and components.

Process control requirements

» Develop and document procedures to plan, monitor, and control your production, installation, and servicing processes.

» Design a record keeping system that monitors and controls process personnel and equipment. Make sure that all important process qualities are monitored and recorded.

» Develop procedures to control the software replication process.

» Develop procedures to control the software release process.

» Develop procedures to control the software installation process.

Product inspection and testing

» Develop procedures to inspect, test, and verify that incoming, in-process, and final products meet all specified requirements. Also ensure that appropriate product inspection and testing records are developed, and that your procedures ensure that these records are properly maintained.

» Develop and document software test plans.

» Develop procedures which ensure that incoming products are not used until you have verified that they meet all specified requirements.

» Develop and document procedures to verify software products and data that are provided by third parties and will be built into your software product. Third parties may include your customers and suppliers.

» Develop procedures which ensure that work in progress meets all requirements before work is allowed to continue.

» Develop procedures which ensure that final products meet all requirements before they are made available for sale.

» Perform software validation tests and software acceptance tests.

» Develop a record keeping system that your staff can use to document all product testing and inspection activities.

Control of inspection equipment

» Develop procedures to control, calibrate, and maintain inspection, measuring, and test equipment used to demonstrate that your products conform to specified requirements (please note that the term equipment includes both hardware and software).

» Use tools, techniques, and equipment to test whether your software products meet specified requirements.

» Develop procedures to ensure that your measurement equipment is appropriate, effective, and secure.

» Develop procedures to calibrate all of your quality-oriented inspection, measuring, and test equipment.

» Develop procedures to calibrate hardware and tools used to test and validate your software products.

Inspection/test status of products

» Develop procedures to control the test status of your products. These procedures should ensure that:

  » each and every product is identified as having passed or failed the required tests and inspections;

  » the test status of each product is documented and respected throughout the production, installation, and servicing process;

  » only products that have passed all tests and inspections are subsequently used or sold to customers (unless an official exception is made); and

  » methods are developed to identify and control the test status of your software products and components.

Control of nonconforming products

» Develop procedures to prevent the inappropriate use of nonconforming products. Also make sure that everyone is notified when your products do not conform to specified requirements.

» Segregate your nonconforming software by placing it into a separate environment.

» Control how software defects and nonconformities are investigated and resolved.

» Develop procedures to control how your nonconforming products are reviewed, reworked, regraded, retested, recorded, and discussed.

» Control the disposition of nonconforming software products and components.
» Retest software products that have been modified.

Corrective and preventive action

» Develop procedures to correct or prevent nonconformities.
» Use configuration management procedures to control corrective and preventive actions that affect software items and products.
» Use document and data control procedures to control corrective and preventive actions that affect software life-cycle processes.
» Develop procedures to ensure that nonconformities are identified and corrected without delay.
» Develop procedures to ensure that potential nonconformities are routinely detected and prevented.
» Develop preventive actions by analyzing the root causes of your nonconformities.
» Develop preventive actions by analyzing unfavorable metric levels and trends.

Handling, storage, and delivery

» Develop and document procedures to handle, store, package, preserve, and deliver your products.
» Develop product handling methods and procedures that prevent product damage or deterioration.
» Your product handling procedures should help prevent damage to your software products and avoid deterioration.
» Designate secure areas to store and protect your products.
» Develop procedures which specify how your products will be placed into storage and removed from storage.
» Develop procedures which specify how your products will be protected from damage or deterioration during storage.
» Develop procedures to control how your software products and items will be stored and protected.
» Store software masters and copies in a secure environment.
» Develop procedures which specify how your products will be monitored and evaluated to detect damage or deterioration while in storage.

» Develop packing, packaging, and marking methods and procedures to protect and control the quality of products and packaging materials.
» Develop methods and procedures to protect and preserve product quality prior to delivery and while the product is still under your control.
» Develop methods to protect and preserve software product quality prior to delivery while the product is still under your control.
» Develop procedures to protect your products after final testing and inspection, and during product delivery.
» Protect your software during delivery.
» Develop and document procedures to preserve product integrity and protect against software viruses.

Control of quality records

» Identify and define the quality information that should be collected.
» Develop a quality record keeping system, and develop procedures to maintain and control it. Develop procedures to:
  » collect and record quality information (create records);
  » file, index, store, and maintain quality records;
  » remove, archive, and destroy old quality records;
  » protect quality records from unauthorized access;
  » prevent records from being altered without approval; and
  » safeguard records from damage or deterioration.
» Software quality records are documents and files that prove that quality activities were performed and quality results were achieved.

Internal quality audit requirements

» Develop internal quality audit procedures which:
  » determine whether quality activities and results comply with written quality plans, procedures, and programs;
  » evaluate the performance of your quality system; and
  » verify the effectiveness of your corrective actions.
» These procedures should also ensure that:
  » audit activities are properly planned;
  » auditors are independent of the people being audited;
  » audit results, corrective actions, and corrective action results and consequences are properly recorded;

» audit conclusions are discussed with the people whose activities and results are being audited, and deficiencies are corrected; and

» audit reports are fed back into the quality system review process.

» Develop an internal audit plan or program for software projects.

Training requirements

» Develop quality training procedures. These procedures must ensure that:

» quality system training needs are identified;

» quality training is provided to those who need it;

» people are able to perform quality system jobs;

» people have the qualifications they need to do the work;

» accurate and appropriate training records are kept; and

» everyone understands how your quality system works.

» Identify the training that will be needed to develop software products and to manage software development projects.

» Identify your training needs by studying how software will be developed and how projects will be managed.

Servicing requirements

» Develop and document quality service procedures. Your procedures should specify how:

» products should be serviced;

» product service activities are reported; and

» the quality of product service is verified.

» Develop procedures to control your software maintenance process.

» Develop plans to control your software maintenance projects.

» Keep a record of your software maintenance activities.

Statistical techniques

» Select the statistical techniques that you will need in order to establish, control, and verify your process capabilities and product characteristics.

» Develop procedures to explain how your techniques should be applied.

» Develop procedures to monitor and control how techniques are used.

» Make sure that all statistical procedures are documented.

» Make sure that proper statistical records are kept.
» Use statistical techniques to analyze the software development process.
» Use statistical techniques to analyze software product characteristics.
» Use statistical techniques to evaluate process and product quality.

ISO 9000–4

ISO 9000–4 explains what a Product Dependability Program is and how it should be managed. The purpose of a Product Dependability Program is to produce products that are reliable and maintainable. Your organization should consider the ISO 9000–4 program if dependability is an important aspect of product quality.

» *Define a Product Dependability Policy*. Start by defining a policy that explains your attitude towards product dependability and which specifies dependability characteristics.
» *Define Functions and Provide Resources*. Define the organizational functions that you will need in order to manage and maintain your product dependability program and ensure that this program has the resources it needs to carry out these functions.
» *Product Dependability Requirements* should be defined by researching customer needs. Therefore, market research procedures are needed.
» *Program Review Procedures* should be developed. Make sure your Product Dependability Program is reviewed regularly by:
  » senior management; and
  » an independent person.
» *Document Every Aspect* of your product dependability program including the procedures used to control and evaluate product dependability.
» *Quantitative and Qualitative Tools*, to analyze and estimate the dependability of products, should be made available to your staff. Also, make sure that these people know how to use these tools.
» *Documents And Records Should Be Maintained*. These documents and records should include:
  » product dependability plans;
  » dependability test instructions and data; and
  » results of dependability analyses and predictions.

» *Set Up An Information System* to track and store product dependability data. Use this data to design and redesign your products and to plan your maintenance activities.

» *Maintain A Master List* of program dependability documents and make sure that only current versions are in circulation.

» *Develop a Product Dependability Plan*. This plan should specify your dependability activities, practices, and resources.

» *Develop Contract Review Procedures*. These procedures must ensure that you and your customers explicitly agree on product dependability expectations and requirements.

» *Prepare Product Specifications* which list availability, reliability, and maintainability performance requirements.

» *Clarify Product Dependability Requirements*. Before you design products, make sure that all product dependability requirements are clarified and that the design will meet these requirements.

» *Develop Product Design and Maintenance Guidelines* to ensure that product dependability requirements are met.

» *Purchased Products Must Meet Dependability Requirements*. Develop procedures to ensure that all products provided by outsiders meet your dependability requirements.

» *Analyze Dependability*. Develop procedures to analyze, predict, and review the dependability of all of your products.

» *Verify Dependability*. Develop procedures to verify and validate product dependability requirements.

» *Calculate Costs*. Develop procedures to calculate product life-cycle costs.

» *Provide Customer Support*. Make sure that your customers know how to operate and maintain your products.

» *Improve Product Dependability*. Develop procedures to improve the dependability of your products.

» *Develop a Feedback System*. Develop procedures to collect product dependability data and gather customer feedback.

GLOSSARY

Internal Audit Manager Competencies Statement

Accessible/approachable – Easy to reach and easy to talk to; responds positively and quickly to customer's calls and requests; is visible and involved on assignments; gives customers first priority and full attention; meets regularly with customers.

Challenges conventional thinking – Is innovative and contributes ideas; challenges the status quo; sees change as a permanent, perpetual process; has vision; has original and lateral thinking.

Coaching/development – Contributes to the development of staff through on-the-job training, coaching, training programs, etc; invests time in staff matters; demonstrates an ability to develop and train key staff.

Commercial performance – Maximizes cost recoveries; controls and negotiates; obtains cost recoveries commensurate with the value of service and resources committed; manages the resources of the internal audit function efficiently.

Commitment to excellence – Sets high standards and achieves them; committed to excellence; works to create continuous improvement in deliverables or work practices.

Communication/influencing/negotiating – Influences others through personal conviction; uses logical/rationale arguments to support a point of view; is assertive; negotiates and resolves issues; is a skilled negotiator.

Conceptual thinking – Demonstrates a capacity to organize and integrate different data into a coherent frame of reference.

Customer service/knowledge (fully shared) – Uses Internal Audit's base of knowledge and experience; takes steps to build own intellectual capital and knowledge of best practice; proactive in translating this into constructive advice (beyond technical compliance) which enables customers to make the best decisions and improve their performance; contributes to Internal Audit's base of knowledge, experience and expertise; shares information internally.

Enthusiasm/motivation – Maintains high energy level, drive, and eagerness to achieve objectives; displays high levels of enthusiasm and energy.

Feedback – Provides staff with timely, honest, and constructive feedback; counsels staff on an ongoing basis.

Flexibility – Maintains effectiveness in different situations; is receptive to new ideas.

Formal presentation – Delivers polished presentations.

Initiative – Takes the initiative on assignments.

Issues identification and problem solving – Deals confidently with complex technical issues; able to solve complex technical problems; arrives at technically correct and innovative solutions; gives advice not opinions.

Job management/productivity – Uses time efficiently, has high productivity; does not procrastinate; uses resources efficiently.

Judgement/decision making – Is prepared to make independent decisions rather than defer; makes quality decisions based on logical assumptions; demonstrates mature and balanced judgement.

Leverage/empowerment – Creates an environment in which staff are empowered; delegates effectively and appropriately; supervises effectively, providing support and resources without interference.

Meetings/interviews – Chairs meetings confidently and effectively, achieving defined objectives; contributes constructively to meetings.

Networking – Generates ideas and contributes to the development or implementation of new strategies.

Oral communication – Explains and expresses views/opinions clearly and confidently; listens carefully to ensure full understanding.

People development and management/leadership/respect – Leads by example; is able to get the best out of a team; achieves recognition as a leader; commands the respect of staff; motivates and challenges the team; is a role model.

Personal effectiveness/integrity/professionalism – Demonstrates extremely high professional standards; is honest and trustworthy.

Planning/organization – Establishes and balances priorities; project manages individual assignments effectively and profitably; manages simultaneous assignments appropriately.

Positive relationships – Develops strong personal relationships with senior management and decision makers; works closely with the customer; becomes a valued member of the management team.

Proactive advice/predicting customer needs – Identifies issues, problems, and needs beyond the focus of specific assignments; introduces tailored solutions; anticipates needs and volunteers advice; is not just reactive.

Progress reporting – Proactively communicates issues/progress to the CEO.

Research and analysis – Ability to research, analyze, organize, and distil data effectively.

Respect for corporate culture – Identifies, understands, and respects corporate culture, needs, motivations, and requirements; uses knowledge to tailor service and advice.

Risk management/quality assurance – Identifies, evaluates, and resolves issues affecting professional risk; plans and manages the assignment to minimize risks; evaluates the significance of issues arising; reviews assignments to ensure quality meets or exceeds professional standards; maintains quality assurance over deliverables.

Social interaction – Able to converse in general terms on a broad range of government business and social issues; is well read and conversant with current issues; able to interact socially at a senior level.

Specialization – Has some recognition as an expert resource in an industry/marketplace.

Task reporting – Completes assignments to the required standards within deadlines and budgets.

Team involvement – Leads/contributes to the team effort; supports others; is willing to be part of the management team and actively contributes to the effective working of the function; participates in social activities.

Teamwork/co-operation – Creates and sustains an environment where participation in the co-operative effort to service external and internal customers is a high priority; consults with, communicates, and builds relationships; shares information.

Technical competence/application of technical knowledge – Demonstrates a high level of current technical skills and expertise; proactive in assessing impact of current and forthcoming technical pronouncements on internal customers.

Technology – Recognizes opportunities for the effective use of microcomputers; manages the use of technology by staff.

Utilization – Uses staff effectively on an individual and on a group basis; balances the workloads of staff.

Value for money – Demonstrated ability to add value; delivers value for money; doesn't let costs get out of hand.

Written expression – Produces clear and succinct reports and correspondence in a polished and professional style; tailors communication to different clients.

Resources

- » Audit and internal control checklist:
    - » general
    - » cash handling and deposits
    - » personnel/payroll records
    - » purchases and disbursements
    - » property and equipment
    - » data processing software/hardware
    - » records retention.

AUDIT AND INTERNAL CONTROL CHECKLIST

The following checklist provides an effective assessment tool in analyzing a company and its performance. It should be noted that individual cases vary and that the checklist is meant to be illustrative of processes rather than an applicable model.

Obviously, careful consideration about the company being audited should be undertaken before developing a similar checklist and applying it.

In the following example checklist, a "no" answer to one of the following questions may indicate the presence of an internal control weakness. This checklist is only a guide, and is not all-inclusive. Therefore, it does not serve as a substitute for the use of audit services.

General

» Do you create, maintain, and make departmental procedure manuals available to your staff?

» Are designations of authority for approval of personnel, payroll, purchasing, and accounts payable transactions reviewed regularly to ensure that appropriate employees have been authorized?

» Are year-end purchases being certified forward to avoid loss of allocated resources and to properly record university liabilities at year-end?

» Are all year-end fiscal close-out procedures followed as indicated by the appropriate authorities?

» Do your key staff have access to the organization's procedures manual?

» Are vehicle logs properly maintained which include date and time of use, driver, name, odometer reading, purpose for which the vehicle was used, and evidence of review by appropriate department personnel?

» Are records for the use of mobile phone services maintained indicating the date of the call, person called and purpose of the call?

Cash handling and deposits

» Are staff members responsible for cash handling and deposits familiar with corporate policies and procedures?

» Are official receipts or cash register tapes issued each time a cash payment is received?
» Are pre-numbered receipts and cash register tapes independently accounted for and controlled?
» Are all voids and copies accounted for?
» Are receipts issued immediately or mail receipt logs maintained for all forms of remittances/collections?
» Are all checks restrictively endorsed upon receipt?
» Are all collections deposited intact in accordance with corporate procedures?
» Are receipts and deposits reconciled monthly with departmental financial statements received from Accounting?
» Are physical transfers of funds documented in writing and receipted by the individual accepting the transfer?
» Are funds physically stored in a safe or equally secure place?
» Are safe combinations changed frequently?
» Is knowledge of safe combinations restricted to employees with a need to know?
» Is the petty cash fund periodically counted without any pre-announcement?
» Are responsibilities for cash receipts and accounts receivable assigned to separate employees?

Personnel/payroll records

» Are staff members responsible for payroll administration familiar with organizational policies and procedures?
» Are the roles of payroll preparation, authorization, certification, and distribution of pay checks separated among different employees in different departmental areas?
» Are timecards checked to ensure accurate entries have been made before they are signed?
» Do timecards and other payroll-related documentation agree with each period's final payroll certification?
» Are formal documentation comparisons of payroll pay lists to the departmental certifications conducted each pay period?
» Are annual and sick leave occurrences entered into the leave system (manual leave reports) in a timely manner?

- » Are annual and sick leave occurrences of the departmental leave keeper entered into the leave system (manual leave reports) by someone other than the leave keeper?
- » Is annual leave authorized in writing before it is taken?
- » Are approved payroll authorizers and certifiers on record with the payroll office?
- » Do supervisors approve overtime before it is incurred?

Purchases and disbursements

- » Are staff members responsible for purchasing and disbursement functions familiar with the organization's Procedures Manual?
- » Are the duties of requisition and purchase order preparation separated from receipt of ordered items and vendor invoice approval?
- » Are purchase requisitions signed by employees specifically authorized to perform this task?
- » Are vendor invoices processed within a reasonable timeframe from the date?
- » Are properly supported travel vouchers processed within 30 days of the travel?
- » Do you maintain all documentation relating to purchases of both goods and services?
- » Are encumbrances and disbursements reconciled monthly with departmental ledgers?
- » Are authorized signatures on file with the payables and disbursements office?
- » Are appropriate discounts offered being taken?
- » Are discount terms highlighted and afforded special handling?
- » Are telephone bills, including those for mobile phones, reviewed and appropriately certified?

Property and equipment

- » Are property identification decals placed in an easily scanned spot and maintained to make the inventory easier?
- » Is surplus equipment secured until properly inventoried and approved for removal?
- » Do you record and submit equipment inventory reports and transfers in a timely manner?

» Are all work areas appropriately secured to deter unauthorized entry?
» Is stolen or missing equipment reported to the police department?
» Is access to departmental storerooms limited?
» Is a form completed and submitted for equipment authorized to be kept off-site?

Data processing software/hardware

» Do you maintain a log of all computer software purchased and take steps to protect the original disks from abuse and damage?
» Do you have a departmental policy against using pirated (stolen) software and do you regularly examine microcomputer hard disks for the presence of illegal software?
» Are your computer systems and peripherals monitored to ensure system security and physical protection?
» Do you make backup copies of appropriate data files on a regular basis?
» Are backups stored in a remote location?

Records retention

» Does your office follow the approved records retention schedule on file with the company's archivist?
» Are annual requests to destroy and discard accumulated records properly filed with the archivist before destroying anything to improve office space and university resource utilization?

Ten Steps to Making Internal Audit and Measurement Work

» Understand the role of audit, measurement, and control.
» Apply internal audit and measurement creatively.
» Incorporate the e-dimension.
» Use information technology auditing.
» Use the Internet as an audit information source.
» Understand the global dimension.
» Harness ISO and build the audit ready company.
» Understand international convergence and legislation.
» Customize the audit and internal control checklist.
» Audit and internal control is a performance enhancing tool, not a fault diagnostic tool.

1. UNDERSTAND THE ROLE OF AUDIT, MEASUREMENT, AND CONTROL

Audit relates to the procedures of analyzing and assessing corporate structures. Measurement means assessing the performance of those organizations against established benchmarks. Control is the mechanisms provided to senior management to enable them to exercise control over corporate activities.

Audit therefore is an invaluable tool in enabling company managers to understand the nature of the operations that they are managing and manage them more effectively. Measurement and control are the tools used by managers to implement their policy directives.

2. APPLY INTERNAL AUDIT AND MEASUREMENT CREATIVELY

Audit and internal measurement is dynamic, not static, and is influenced by the competitive pressures in the marketplace as well as moves of competitors.

In a larger sense, audit is affected by two external factors – changes in the regulatory environment, and changes in the technological environment.

Technology impacts companies and their operations. However, technology also impacts the audit profession and the ability to pool and analyze information more effectively than in the past.

3. INCORPORATE THE E-DIMENSION

The rise of e-technology has impacted the world of audit and internal control as it meets e-business. Audit and measurement therefore needs to become proactive in the analysis and assessment of companies operating in the new e-paradigms.

Similarly, the Internet as an information gathering and idea exchanging tool should be assessed and used by auditors in the undertaking of their tasks. Incorporating the e-dimension will enable audit and measurement to operate in a synergistic community, tapping an infinite pool of expertise, as opposed to operating in isolation.

4. USE INFORMATION TECHNOLOGY AUDITING

Audit and measurement's rigorous disciplines offer the possibility of extending systematic and effective assessment procedures in the diagnostic of organizational processes and definition of structures and business models. Audit and measurement can therefore help in optimizing business structures and procedures before passing to the next crucial step of defining IT architectures and e-business architectures. Use audit and measurement, therefore, to assist in the construction of IT systems, which enhance (as opposed to constrain) business operations.

5. USE THE INTERNET AS AN AUDIT INFORMATION SOURCE

The Internet unites hitherto disparate and hence non-competing entities. Audit and measurement can discuss generic problems and air solutions which are of relevance to the auditor's mission. Proactive use of the Internet as a reference and information tool can also be supplemented by participation in industry and audit discussion forums enabling pertinent and hard-hitting recommendations benefiting from a solid implementation track record to be suggested.

6. UNDERSTAND THE GLOBAL DIMENSION

The rise of the integrated multinational or financial services entity means that the role of audit and measurement is now transnational. It is therefore crucial to understand the new internationalized context, not only in the sense that companies are now cross-border, but in the sense that the regulatory and compliance regimes governing them are also cross-border.

It is therefore crucial that the audit function be cognizant of the fact that business pressures, regulatory imperatives, and technological evolution are global in nature and that the diagnostics effected incorporate these elements.

7. HARNESS ISO AND BUILD THE AUDIT READY COMPANY

ISO offers the advantages of legitimizing processes and reassuring investors as well as customers. Implementing ISO also offers the possibility of creating and implementing rational structures within the organization. This development is obviously linked closely in hand to that of internal audit and measurement. It is therefore paramount to consider the importance in ISO implementation as an ally of effective audit and measurement implementation.

8. UNDERSTAND INTERNATIONAL CONVERGENCE AND LEGISLATION

As the world economy internationalizes and becomes increasingly interdependent and follows the models implemented by entities such as the OECD and WTO, it is important that audit and internal control entities understand the impact these transnational factors have on the operations and competitive environment of the organization. It is often too easy to assess the company internally, in isolation, rather than against the backdrop of international convergence and legislation. Becoming aware of these elements not only will result in more effective audit and recommendations, but will also place the auditor ahead of instead of behind the curve.

9. CUSTOMIZE THE AUDIT AND INTERNAL CONTROL CHECKLIST

All audit procedures reside on the systematic examination and evaluation of organizations. These are typically effected via checklists. It is crucial for the auditor to understand that these models are guidelines and need to be customized in function of the nature of the entity being audited. Checklists therefore need to be customized in function of the nature of the entity but also in function of external macro elements such as technology development, business environment changes, and legislative changes.

10. AUDIT AND INTERNAL CONTROL IS A PERFORMANCE ENHANCING TOOL, NOT A FAULT DIAGNOSTIC TOOL

Audit and internal control and measurement exist to improve, rationalize, and enhance organizational performance. It is therefore crucial that auditors stress that their discipline is a tool for management to enhance operations, improve quality control, and achieve competitive edge and information flow rather than being a fault diagnostic and blame allocation tool. Clearly stating this objective at the outset of the audit process should ensure that the flow of information essential to an effective audit process is not impaired.

Frequently Asked Questions (FAQs)

Q1: What is an audit?

A: See Chapter 2 – What is internal control?

Q2: What is an e-audit?

A: See Chapter 4 – Audit and internal control meets e-business and Internet as information source.

Q3: What are the various types of audit in an organization?

A: See Chapter 7 – Types of audit.

Q4: I want to implement an audit and control process in an organization. How do I go about it?

A: See Chapter 7 – Internal audit.

Q5: What is an ISO 9000 certification, and why is it important?

A: See Chapter 8 – What is ISO 9000 and Why is ISO 9000 important?

Q6: I want to implement ISO 9000 certification in my company. How do I do this?

A: See Chapter 8 – How does ISO 9000 work?.

Q7: How is international convergence likely to affect my business?

A: See Chapter 10 – Understand international convergence and legislation.

Q8: What is the difference between audit and e-audit?

A: See Chapter 4 – Audit and internal control meets e-business.

Q9: How do I find out more about the subject?

A: See Chapter 4 – Internet as information source.

Q10: What are the origins of modern auditing?

A: See Chapter 1 – What is audit and internal control?

Index

addresses, Internet 14, 22
advisory services 3
agencies 12
Amazon.com 26
appraisal concept 3
assets, derivatives 31-2
assurance concept 3
audit committees 33, 36, 46-7
audit manager 2-3, 78-82
audit models 40-41, 43, 48-52
audit trail 47-8

banks/banking 9
   deposit guarantee scheme 12-13
   Internet address warning 14
   OCC guidance (USA) 13-14
   risk management 31
Barings Bank 9, 12
best practice survey 17
board of directors 32-3, 36
business failure 30
business units 37

case studies 17, 39-52
cash management 84-5
CEO *see* chief executive officer
certification 56
CFO *see* chief financial officer

checklists 41-2, 84-7, 92
chief executive officer (CEO) 36-7
chief financial officer (CFO) 37
Committee of Sponsoring
   Organizations (COSO) 30-38
communication 34
competencies statement 78-82
competitive edge 27, 54
compliance audits 51
concepts 3-4, 54-78
conferences 50-51
conglomerates 27-8
consulting services 3
contracts 31-2, 61, 67-8
control activities 34
control environment 31-3
controller responsibilities 37
controls, types of 48-9
COSO *see* Committee of Sponsoring
   Organizations
creativity 90
Customer Relationship Management
   (CRM) 26
customer services 79

data control 70, 87
decision making 80

definitions   2, 8–10
derivatives   30–38
design control   61, 68–70
detective controls   48–9
Directorate-General for Financial
    Control   43–4
directors   32–3, 36
disbursements   86
discussion lists, Internet   16–17
documentation
    see also International Organization
        for Standardization
    corrective controls   49
    technical standards   21
domain name *see* addresses
double gearing   28

e-technology   4, 16–17, 26, 90
effectiveness   8, 12–13, 52
efficiency   8–9
Enron Corporation   9
equipment   63, 86–7
EU *see* European Union
European Commission   27–8, 42–3
European Union (EU)   27–8, 40–52
evaluation   59
ex-ante auditing models   40–41
excessive leveraging   28

failure   30
fieldwork   50
financial aspects
    audits   44–5, 51
    checklist, financial control   41–2
    conglomerates   27–8
    contracts   31–2
Financial Services Action Plan   27
France   40
fraud   13
frequently asked questions (FAQs)
    95–6

Gap Analysis   56
gearing   28
glossary   78–82
governance concept   3–4
government agencies   12
grants   45

handling products   64–5, 74–5
Hawke, John D. Jr   13
human resources   17

identifiers   62, 71–2
independence   46–7
information   22, 34, 91
information systems audits   52
information technology (IT)   18–22,
    91
    see also e-technology; Internet
inspections   63–4, 72–3
Institute of Internal Auditors   2–3,
    44, 46
internal control
    checklists   41–2, 84–7
    COSO Framework   32–5
    definitions   2–3, 8–10
    derivatives   30–38
    e-business   16–17, 90
    effectiveness   8, 13
    efficiency   8–9
    European Union   40–43, 47–8
    programs   12–14
    risk   3–4
    roles/responsibilities   36–8, 42–3
    ten steps   90
    types   48–9
*Internal Control - Integrated
    Framework* (COSO)   30–38
The Internal and External Audits
    (OCC)   13
International Organization for
    Standardization (ISO)   55
    ISO 9000   54–78

global issues   27
information   22
internal control   10
publications   57-8
quality control   4-5, 54-5
ten steps   91-2
ISO 9000-1   58-60
ISO 9000-2   60-66
ISO 9000-3   66-77
ISO 9000-4   77-8
Internet
see also information technology
addresses   14, 22
auditing   16-17
information   22
ten steps   90-91
investigative audits   52
ISO *see* International Organization for
Standardization
IT *see* information technology

Joint Forum on Financial
Conglomerates (1999)   27

key aspects
concepts   54-78
frequently asked questions   95-6
glossary   78-82
resources   84-7
ten steps   90-93

legislation   27-8, 92
leveraging   28
lists, Internet discussion   16-17
LISTSERV   16-17
Luxembourg   43

management
see also internal control
audit managers   2-3
competency   33, 78-82
derivatives   30-38

European Union audits   40-41
policy formulation   37
monitoring, derivatives   34-6
motivation   79

Netherlands   43
networking   80
nonconforming products   64, 73-4

objectives, audits   13-14
Office of the Comptroller of the
Currency (OCC)   12-14
operational audits   51
oversight, directors   32-3
overview, ISO 9000   57-8

packing products   74-5
payroll records   85-6
performance   79, 92-3
performance audits   45
personnel records   85-6
planning   49-50
Portugal   43
pre-audit research   16-17
preparation   49
preventive controls   48
problem solving   80
processes   59, 63, 72
product control
design requirements   68-70
identification   62, 71-2
inspection/testing   72-3
nonconforming   64, 73-4
packaging/delivery   64-5, 71,
74-5
quality standards   58
suitability   62
Product Dependability Programs
77-8
professionalism   80
property   86-7

public financial control checklist 41–2

publications, ISO 9000 57–8

purchasing 62, 70–71, 86

quality control 10
    see also International Organization
        for Standardization

recommendations 16–17, 51

records 65, 75, 85–7

registration 56

regulatory agencies 12

reporting 17, 49–52

requirements, ISO 9000–1 58–60

research, pre-audit 16–17

resources 45, 84–7

responsibilities 36–8, 42–3, 60, 66–7

reviews, audit 51

risk
    audit programs 13–14
    controls 3–4
    derivatives 30–38
    management 3, 81

roles 36–8, 42–3

Romania 40

SDLC *see* system development life cycle

security 21

self-assessment 37

senior management *see* management

servicing 66, 76

software 66–77

specialization 81

stakeholders 4

standards 18–22, 54–78
    see also International Organization
        for Standardization

start-up companies 27, 54

statistical techniques 66, 76–7

storing products 64–5, 74–5

subcontractors 62

Supplements, COSO Framework 31

surveys 17

system development life cycle (SDLC) 18–20

systems, ISO 9000 56–7

teamwork 81

technical standards 20–22

tenders 45

terminology changes 3–4

testing 63–4, 72–3

tracing 47–8, 71–2

training 65, 76, 79

transaction checking 44–5

United Kingdom 41, 43

USA Office of the Comptroller of the Currency (OCC) 12–14

Usenet 16, 22

value-for-money audits *see* performance audits

Websites 22

Printed and bound by CPI Group (UK) Ltd, Croydon, CR0 4YY

14/04/2025

14656894-0001

Printed and bound in the UK by
CPI Antony Rowe, Eastbourne